14.95
12/6/04

Just Add Management

Seven Steps to Creating a Productive
Workplace and Motivating Your
Employees in Challenging Times

FARZAD DIBACHI
RHONDA LOVE DIBACHI

McGraw-Hill

New York   Chicago   San Francisco   Lisbon   London   Madrid
Mexico City   Milan   New Delhi   San Juan   Seoul
Singapore   Sydney   Toronto

We especially want to thank our good friend, Joan Hamilton, for all of her assistance, encouragement, and advice. She knows, more than anyone else, that it would not have been possible without her.

Contents

Foreword by William J. Raduchel, CTO of AOL Time Warner   vii

Acknowledgments   ix

Introduction: The Myth of "It"   1

Chapter 1: The Knowledge Work Murk   7

Chapter 2: Getting the Basics Straight   27

Chapter 3: Inspiring and Rewarding Employees   41

Chapter 4: The Vision Thing   61

Chapter 5: Doing What Matters   75

Chapter 6: Figuring Out How to Do It Right Every Time   95

Chapter 7: Progress Tracking   123

Chapter 8: Working Smarter   145

Chapter 9: The Diba Diaries   165

Chapter 10: The Transparency Payback   189

Appendix: Checklists and Templates   201

Endnotes   221

Bibliography   223

Index   225

Foreword

WHEN I STARTED WRITING SOFTWARE more than 40 years ago, it was an intellectual curiosity of limited practical application. After all, what could you usefully do with much less computing power than is in a modern digital watch? How times have changed! There are very few—if any—material business projects today that don't have crucial dependence on software and information technology. Firms have evolved from informal networks of informal systems communicating using imprecise protocols to complex, formal networks of complex, formal systems communicating using precise protocols not only within the firm but with customers, suppliers, and regulators. A firm, after all, is only an information system at its core. John Kenneth Galbraith foresaw all this in his seminal *The New Industrial State* nearly 35 years ago.

Every company has its mavens, and these mavens can turn the corporate power structure upside down. In my experience, technology befuddles many executives and leads them to managing it incorrectly. There are many reasons for this, and I still find myself confused and bemused when I witness it. Personal computers have turned millions into self-proclaimed technology experts, and firms that would insist on hiring a litigator with world-class experience for a major lawsuit are more than willing to hand a complex system implementation to an often-talented, but amateur, amateur. Partly it is because technology experts frequently come across as difficult to fathom and manage. And partly it is because business executives don't like most of the laws of physics that apply to technology and therefore often want the impossible. The maven phenomenon can also occur in nontechnical, but specialized fields such as international marketing or corporate finance—any realm where the knowledge worker's job mechanics are beyond the ken of a manager. Tales of U.S. executives' hiring a foreign manager primarily on the person's ability to speak English rather than a track record of making money in that market are all too familiar.

As a result, in countless situations a shaky détente has been reached: Tell the mavens what you need, leave them alone, and pray they deliver (and augment that prayer with results-oriented compensation). Of course, they often don't deliver much more than tales of late and over-budget projects. Even more commonly, but less understood, project teams often delete features to make the date, so you don't get what you expected. By cutting corners in software in particular, you end up with a product that is less an asset and more a liability than anyone had intended.

Why does this happen? First and foremost, it does not happen because the technologists or other mavens are somehow flawed. In my almost universal experience, they are among the best, hardest-working and most dedicated employees in the company. When you build systems, truth is an absolute and ambiguity is death. Second, it does not happen because the business objectives are bad, although that is sometimes the case. Executives get to where they are because they have skills and abilities, and they usually make the right calls.

As do the authors, I believe so many projects collapse because the interface between the business executives and the mavens is flawed—the mavens are managed poorly. They talk past each other. Meaning well, they end up doing harm. I don't believe in simple management formulas, but I do believe every good executive has to have a theory of how to do his or her job. What Farzad and Rhonda lay out here is the foundation for effective, results-oriented technology management, and I commend it to all with that need—which today means just about everybody in any kind of organization.

William J. Raduchel
Executive Vice President
Chief Technical Officer
AOL Time Warner, Inc.

Acknowledgments

W<small>E THANK OUR FRIENDS</small>, colleagues, and most of all our customers for helping us understand the many ways of managing knowledge workers. Thanks to everyone at Niku, especially Mark Moore, Stjepan Morovich, Jules Ehrlich, and Kurt Steinle. Thanks to every person at every company who participated in all of our conversations that we had during the course of this project. Special thanks go to Terry Ash, Robert Atkinson, Tom Berquist, John Birge, Carol Bobbe, Volkhard Bregulla, Phil Brown, Stephen Cooke, John Elliott, Dave Ewert, Frank Gill, Joe Gillach, Harriet Girdley, Arnold Goto, Fred Jewell, Brendan Kennedy, Licia Knight, John Lambeth, Geoffrey Lawson, Bill Lehrmann, Bill Leonard, LeeAnne Lewis, David Meridew, Leslie Mullis, Jo Myland, Dave Phillips, Bill Raduchel, Dave Raspallo, Stuart Read, Debbie Russell, Steve Saba, Bob Schwartz, Nancy Simonson, Ed Soladay, Bill Stewart, Peter Thompson, Dave Veach, Bernhard Vieregge, Maynard Webb, Richard Whelchel, Jeremy Wilkes, and Paul Yaron for being so generous with their time and sharing so many useful insights.

INTRODUCTION
The Myth of "It"

Thomas FALL OF ENRON, the Houston-based energy-trading company that flamed out in 2001, is an amazing debacle. Reading about its decline, we were struck particularly by the words of the company's former CEO Jeff Skilling as quoted in a *BusinessWeek* article: "There were two kinds of people in the world: those who got 'it' and those who didn't."[1] Ultimately, though, nobody—not even the company's chairman or its board of directors—could explain or justify the shaky and sketchy offshore and off-book partnerships Skilling and his team created that crashed and brought Enron down with them. Enron's financial staff operated in a maverick and unaccountable fashion. As the stock value plunged into the pennies, everybody got "it." "It" was a house of cards.

Business is currently recovering from its rocket ride through the get-it decade. Thank God it's over. The get-it cults that sprung up in the supposed New Economy exacerbated a problem that's been plaguing business for decades—namely, the challenge of managing workers whose output isn't measured in the goods they produce or the sales they book, but rather in the value they create by manipulating knowledge. It's an arena where many workers pride themselves on the creativity and individual solutions they bring to their daily challenges. They chafe at attempts to make them accountable for their work. Whether the business is books or electronic trading of electricity, they like to talk in terms of cleverness, thinking outside the box, and the qualitative genius they bring to the endeavor. Trust us, they say. We get it.

We heard it from high-wire-artist executives like Skilling. We heard it from tech types who couldn't be bothered to explain what they were doing in terms a normal person could understand. But the most damaging fallout of this swaggering sentiment was its grip on managers of millions of knowledge workers. It's very difficult to manage knowledge workers. It takes sensitivity and flexibility and smarts—but it also requires enforcing basic business processes whether the field is finance, law, business development, customer service, marketing, options trading, or information technology. Unfortunately, as the get-it chants grew among the knowledge legions embracing all kinds of new technology and fueled by a booming economy, managers surrendered and gave up. They began relying on heroics to get the job done, rather than standard, repeatable processes. And like Skilling, many developed a taste for risk that ultimately betrayed them.

Enron's collapse is just one example of the fallout. Scores of Wall Street traders and analysts are under the microscope for questionable practices that developed in a largely unsupervised, booming market. IT managers who were given blank checks to do whatever "it" took to bring a company into the Internet Age are now digging out from under a mountain of poorly understood, often dysfunctional technology they bought in a panic. The dot.com legions whose profits-optional ideas were supposed to reinvent the universe all claimed to "get it." Billions in invested capital later, such names as Webvan, Excite, and Yahoo are now more synonymous with broken dreams than with revolutionary business ideas. Humility has come at a heavy price.

All these situations are dramatic management failures. In a more insidious form of failure, however, a lack of good management means businesses large and small around the world continue to experience lags in productivity, delays in their responsiveness to new opportunities, duplicative and unproductive initiatives, wasted resources, and a generalized frustration. Intensifying the problem are the complexities introduced by the advent of far-flung virtual teams and the sheer volume and velocity of information flowing through even the most mundane business operations these days.

Farzad's background is in software development. He's managed divisions at Tandem Computer and Oracle Corporation, and he has started up two software companies. Rhonda is an operational executive who has managed some of the most challenging knowledge workers of all—software programmers—with great success. Because of the nature of the systems with which we've been involved, we have unusual insight into the habits and culture of the knowledge workers in today's business world. We also have some battle scars: In Farzad's last startup, his flirtation with "management by getting out of the way" (illuminated in some detail in Chapter 9) didn't work. The experience changed the way we'll do business forever.

We have written this book because of a confluence of two strongly held beliefs. The first is that technology has evolved to an exciting point. In the last couple of decades two enormous business sectors—manufacturing and sales—have experienced tremendous new efficiencies and planning capabilities thanks to so-called enterprise software programs designed for *enterprise resource planning* (ERP) and *customer relationship management* (CRM). Now gains of similar magnitude are imminent in the far less quantitative knowledge workplace as well. Even more exciting, these methods stand to finally deliver the long-promised benefits of using systems to help people work smarter too.

Our second belief is that, to reach this last major productivity frontier to take advantage of these new tools, managers of knowledge workers must take charge. Today, too many managers of knowledge workers are paralyzed by myths about what it takes to get and keep the best people. Managers often behave as if they are afraid of their own workers. They are stumped by such laments as, How can you attack productivity in an environment in which quality, not quantity, is important? How can you hold a legal department facing a wide array of unique situations to productivity metrics? How can you subject a marketing strategy group charged with developing breakthrough, creative campaigns to such notions as process and on-time delivery? How can employees who never directly see a customer be expected to think about how their work affects the people who pay their salaries?

The more the economy contracts, the more imperative it becomes that businesses not neglect any component of their cost or productivity equations. Service and middle-company functions represent an enormous chunk of American business, employing almost 60 percent of the workforce.[2] However, studies have shown that while manufacturing productivity has increased by over 50 percent in the past 10 years, productivity in the internal service sectors has remained flat.[3]

Knowledge workers' productivity is a huge competitiveness issue. Attacking it goes way beyond just hiring smart people. The best people in the world, if not properly managed, cannot produce the results it takes to drive an enterprise forward on a consistent basis. What most of us need are systems and strategies for managing and maximizing the value of workers who occupy the vast middle ground between lousy and brilliant. We need approaches to managing our knowledge workers that focus them on doing what matters in a timely way. Only after the basics are achieved can we afford to invite the A+ employees—a minority in any mid- to large-sized enterprise, and probably in most small companies—to dazzle us with their cutting-edge ideas and pursue high-risk–high-reward endeavors independently.

What we have learned in the last several years of developing and marketing a software suite designed to help companies in nearly every industry, from manufacturers of pharmaceuticals to motorcycles, is that there is a great desire out there to turbocharge the knowledge workforce but there is also a lot of confusion about how to do it. In hundreds of hours of conversations with customers, we have learned that executives and managers are pulling out their hair in frustration. They don't know what their knowledge workers are doing. They can't quantitatively measure their progress. They don't have a clear picture at any point in time of how things are going, whether projects are truly on track, and whether resources are being deployed on the projects that really matter. These knowledge gaps lead to all kinds of related problems: Managers can't justify their budgets, they can't take advantage of new opportunities quickly or respond to problems or crises effectively, and they can't even scale back their operations when times demand it, because they don't know who's doing what.

This book can help managers turbocharge the knowledge workplace. Whether you are a CEO or a manager deep in an organization, the prescription to help you better understand and drive your organization is the same: Demand accountability and maturity from workers, and systematically organize the knowledge workplace to start delivering more consistently, more efficiently, and more predictably. We are hopeful that our dual perspectives—as a CEO and as an operational executive—will provide both a practical and realistic sense of how to run an accountable organization in which senior executive "drive-bys" are rare and in which knowledge workers focus on doing what matters and on doing it right.

What we outline in this book is a two-step process designed to achieve a critical corporate goal: transparency. Transparency exists when every member of an enterprise understands what his or her role in the greater scheme is; understands how his or her work influences the success of the enterprise; makes good decisions based on priorities set at a high level; and taps into the knowledge assets of the company in order to achieve corporate goals.

Achieving transparency first demands that managers establish and enforce a mature, professional workplace culture focused on results. We call it *adult supervision*.

Second, the adults need to use time-tested, proven management techniques that too often are ignored in the knowledge environment. We call that *accountability management*. Managers need to set and broadcast priorities. They need to agree upon and enforce processes. They need to track employees' progress and make them accountable. And they need to support this accountability management system with knowledge tools that provide accurate, timely business data that help the organization work smarter. These techniques provide the mechanics of visibility—data-driven insight into who's doing what, and how they're doing.

The first three chapters of our book speak to the cultural underpinnings of an accountable, productivity-oriented workplace. We'll run through some realities and myths of today's knowledge workplace. We'll introduce you to some of the archetypes who populate knowledge workplaces such as Amadeus, the artiste; Jock who wants to "just do it"; Darth Maul, the Sith Lord, who says little and may save your bacon— or go postal. While we have some fun with the stereotypical characters and behaviors that lurk in the knowledge workplace, we believe that managers must set the right tone in the office for every employee, every day. Only then will employees be primed to embrace transparency, a state of high alert inside a knowledge organization in which every employee develops a sense of the big picture.

We'll spend the second half of the book focused on the key tactical steps you can take to organize and attack inefficiencies in the knowledge workplace: portfolio alignment, process development, progress tracking, and knowledge management. You can use the sample worksheets in the appendix to help you in this mission, or you can download electronic versions of the worksheets off our Web site at www.niku.com.

A mature organizational philosophy is crucial to getting companies back on track. For its next leap forward, business needs to reconnect with some basic fundamentals that have been lost in all the hype and foment of the last few years. Without adults in charge, all the nifty tools are just expensive toys for technocrats and child prodigy computer geeks. We are going to lay out a method for you to marry brilliantly simple management concepts proven to work, with tools that will give your enterprise wings.

CHAPTER

1

The Knowledge Work Murk

In this chapter we discuss the knowledge workplace, the business world's last major productivity frontier. We sketch some new realities of this technology-savvy and information-rich business arena, and we expose some of the myths that prevent managers from demanding the appropriate accountability from this workforce.

THE CHIEF INFORMATION OFFICER of a large financial services company came to us recently with a story the poor bloke thought was unusual. We'll call him Chuck.[1] A couple of years ago, Chuck landed what he thought was going to be his dream job. The firm he was joining had enjoyed a lot of positive notoriety in a very hot sector. It was a big step up from his last position—he'd be managing more people, for more markets, from a posh office in a Manhattan skyscraper.

He stepped out of the elevator with a spring in his step on his first day and was met by his boss, the chief operations officer (COO), in the corridor. His boss hurriedly pulled him into a conference room and shut the door. The COO admitted he was nervous about a certain project. It was known as the "Decimalization Project," or "D Project." The major U.S. stock exchanges were going to switch from fractional reporting to decimal reporting in early 2001. The company had only a few more months to complete the retrofit of its trading systems and client reporting systems. The stakes were huge: The company needed to make this deadline in order to stay in business after the switch. The COO told Chuck that he needed to guarantee the D Project would come in on time.

His top priority now crystal clear, Chuck went off to find his office.

Chuck began asking his reports a short list of simple questions: Give me a list of everything we're working on around the world. I want to know what kind of financial and personnel resources we're deploying on each of these initiatives. And I need the completion targets. His intention was to evaluate the resource deployment and move bodies to the highest-priority initiatives.

Chuck's new domain included over 1000 of the firm's employees—the lion's share of its personnel resources. Immediately, half of his reports lined up outside his door toting *PowerPoint* presentations. These slides carried all kinds of information. Literally. There were in-depth explorations of the obvious that took 45 minutes to review. There were market research reports and morale-boosting slides full of slogans. They told him about the cultural idiosyncrasies of foreign offices, and reminded him of the firm's access to great seats for the Knicks' games. They handed him incomplete lists of names of people working on initiatives. They handed him spreadsheets providing a crystal clear view of what the company agreed to spend 8 months ago—but no expenses pegged to actual outlays spent on initiatives to date, nor estimates of what it would take to complete them.

That was half of his organization. The other half of his organization didn't respond at all, and when he went to them, "They were surly," recalled Chuck. They seemed to resent the questions. When he mentioned the D Project, some of them openly snickered and said they wouldn't touch it with a 10-foot pole. Yet, as he looked around his operation every day, he saw no slackers or loafers. Everyone looked busy, some to the point of red-eyed exhaustion.

After a week of this, Chuck was dumbfounded. Nobody could give him a list of initiatives, resources, and completion targets. Nobody had a meaningful sense of the big picture. Those above him referred vaguely to the need to kick some ass . . . (We like to call this kind of shallow, unhelpful, often barked advice a " CEO drive-by shooting.")

Those below him were mired in the details and were responding like firefighters to every request from anyone up the ladder. They were running around in circles, not getting anything finished. There was no widely shared sense of corporate priorities. Chunks of initiatives were described simply as in "development phase" in the charts ostensibly designed to keep everyone on track. Some of those "phases" had gone on for months.

And the decimalization clock ticked away. The COO was looking to Chuck for a timeline and a guarantee, but Chuck could not get a straight answer to whether the internal decimalization project was on schedule or whether it needed more resources.

Managers would reply: "More resources? Sure, I'd love to have more resources. I didn't realize that was in the budget."

The budget wasn't the question. The question was: What do you need to bring this in on time? The managers had no idea.

Without any big-picture sense of where they were and what they needed, his managers could not guarantee to Chuck that the deadline was achievable. What was he to do? The COO was looking to him to deliver the D Project in time for the market switch. He couldn't get anyone in his organization to say that it was possible or to show him a believable plan to get there. So Chuck had to bring in a third party for over half a million dollars to analyze the efforts and act as a SWAT team to shore up cracks in the plan.

In the end, the decimalization project barely came in on time, and it came in with a hefty price tag because of the detective work required to get internal efforts in shape, additional consultant fees, and additional people the company had to deploy to make it happen.

Chuck was convinced he'd joined the most dysfunctional organization in town. We assured him it was just another day at the office in the knowledge workplace.

What Is the Knowledge Workplace?

The knowledge workplace is the vast array of work and services inside companies that can make or break an organization but that are not related to manufacturing or sales. In those arenas, output, productivity, and success can be expressed in very specific metrics such as sales, or low defect ratios, or gross production numbers.

The output of the knowledge workplace, however, tends to be far more difficult to quantify and describe. Knowledge workers are sometimes erroneously thought of as just technical, heads-down types who work on a keyboard all day. In fact, knowledge workers include a wide variety of functional specialists who perform services. Hypermeticulous attorneys. Groovy, multiply pierced advertising copywriters. Analysts trying to match up the nuts and bolts of a business with its prospects. Business development executives who spend all their time in the field looking for interesting possibilities. Financial people closing the quarter's books and assembling complex reports. Legions of programmers. What they have in common is that their work tends to be grounded in the gathering, analysis, manipulation, transformation, and presentation of information. What they also have in common is their enormous collective impact: Knowledge workers make up almost 60 percent of the workforce.[2]

The knowledge workplace also often is characterized by teams working on activities that require multiple contributions. For example, a goal is articulated, a team is assembled, a challenge is formulated—and then there is a murky period of waiting and percolating. Ideally, it's followed by the realization that the efforts of a team have gelled into a compelling, successful initiative or service or deal or campaign or strategy. These may include a comarketing deal with a major company. A blockbuster computer game. A new recruiting plan. A fully subscribed investment partnership. A 24 percent reduction in customer complaints.

Or sometimes it's followed by a big mess. Just as common is the discovery that an organization has just wasted precious time, human capital, and financial resources on a poorly defined activity, an impossible dream, or a program of dubious value, in which efforts were wasted and vision and reality were going in opposite directions.

What separates the first scenario, the successful one, from the second, we believe, is management. Management can't always overcome a bad idea, but it can spot one early and change the direction or end the initiative before vast amounts of money and time are wasted. Successful companies find a way to more consistently deliver knowledge-based work and manage business value than unsuccessful companies. That sounds obvious. But the fact is that best practices of those successful companies, and the mechanisms used in those successes, have not been embraced widely. Across the landscape of business, the productivity gains of knowledge workers have dramatically lagged improvements in manufacturing productivity for decades. Over just the last 10 years, for example, studies show manufacturing productivity has increased by over 50 percent, while service productivity has remained flat.[3]

So, are knowledge workers already operating at some prime level of efficiency? No. Look at Chuck's Decimalization Project. This was not a dysfunctional organization barely hanging on. This was a vibrant business that had made dramatic inroads into lots of exciting new segments of financial services. Within the past year, this company had entered into five new international trading markets. This was a thriving and dynamic organization that was attracting fresh talent, like Chuck. It was supporting a growing business model. It was responding to new challenges. But the D Project exposed to Chuck the company's disorganized, unaccountable underpinnings that he grew to realize characterized its entire culture.

We spoke with Chuck about 4 months after the completion of the decimalization project. Chuck was only then starting to recover from the effort it took to manage that monster. He wanted to know if Niku could help him get some visibility into his organization across the board. Chuck had discovered that his people were good at developing new products, where it's easy to establish a sense of teamwork and esprit de corps and a clear goal. But that's a honeymoon activity. Long-term success is about keeping the excitement going while you're also divvying up the household chores, rocking cranky babies to sleep at 2 A.M., and agreeing to live within your means.

Chuck couldn't even begin to manage toward a balanced, productive state because basic questions could not be answered: Who was doing what? What will suffer if we remove the Alpha team's current responsibilities and shift them to the D Project? How many team members' initiatives are close to completion? Which long-range efforts we can safely postpone?

The Decimalization Project, like a number of challenges Chuck's group was facing, was not rocket science. But it involved managing workers who had to be forced to work as a team, share information, and execute their tasks in a serial fashion so the project could move forward. That's where things broke down. This project wasn't creative, ultracool stuff. It was tedious infrastructure work. There were other things many of the employees would rather do, many of them off on their own where they didn't have to meet schedules and answer to the guys in suits. And because there was no central repository for information tracking and monitoring the progress of this project, nobody had a handle on how far the teams had progressed—or whether they'd meet their deadlines.

Sadly, Chuck's is a common lament. Knowledge managers are not getting the visibility they need into their organizations for two reasons: First, they haven't established a mature, professional culture. This has been a get-it culture, and those who have believed they had "it" considered it beneath them to report on any regular basis in any regular way how things were going. Second, managers buy into the fallacy that the same management processes used in quantitative fields such as product design and manufacturing won't work in the knowledge arena because every task is unique. In companies like Chuck's, there is an appalling lack of information on priorities and progress and little information about who is doing what and for what reason. Without this basic information, managers like Chuck find it almost impossible to make the basic decisions necessary to run their organizations.

Management Challenges in the Knowledge Workplace

In our careers, we have worked on initiatives that were designated high priority inside such major companies as General Electric, Tandem Computer, Oracle Corporation, and Arthur Young. We say "designated" because despite all the slogans and CEO drive-bys, it's extremely common for knowledge work to be managed like some kind of artists' colony, where managers assemble a team, throw out a challenge, hope for the best, and return shortly before the deadline, holding their breath and fingering their rosary beads. That's bad enough, but an additional problem is that nobody locks the door to the colony. After issuing the orders, it's also perfectly common for wave after wave of senior executives to come knocking, asking for help and attention from individual team members for all manner of other activities and initiatives, rationalizing the interruptions to the big initiatives with the assurance that this "won't take much time."

When you are tempted to indulge in drive-bys like "Fix the Web site. It stinks," remember that if senior executives plucked workers off an assembly line at random times and asked them to perform ill-defined, low-level tasks, it would probably take less than 24 hours for all hell to break loose: The decline in widget production would expose this problem, and the behavior would stop. But since knowledge work takes time and the workers aren't asked to be accountable on any given day, interruptions and tangential work can suck the life out of an initiative.

These challenges are widely perceived and painfully experienced by thousands of companies. In fact, improving the management of knowledge workers has been designated as one of the most significant modern business challenges by management gurus such as Peter Drucker, who has stated that management's most important contribution during the last century was that manual workers in manufacturing increased their productivity 50 times. Drucker thinks that management's most important contribution for this century will be to raise the productivity of knowledge workers by a similar, staggering amount.[4]

A poorly managed knowledge workplace can become like Peter Pan's Island of Lost Boys. The knowledge workers are often very smart, very motivated, hard-working people. But despite conventional wisdom that those qualities are sufficient, when they're left on their own, they often become frustrated at the lack of clear direction and well-articulated priorities. These employees adopt a resentful independence, convinced that they are misunderstood and underappreciated. They work on the tasks that most interest them, and because they do have specialized skills and knowledge much of the time, it's very difficult to sort out what many of them are doing on a daily basis. "Working on stuff," "analyzing these numbers," "doing research," are all truthful descriptions of their activities, sadly just as truthful when they are doing those things for high-value initiatives as for low-value interruptions or even actions unrelated to their job—like developing ideas they believe will impress the bosses and get them out of their current job, communicating with friends, or playing games. If management has not used a disciplined approach to monitoring their time and progress, entire initiatives can go up in flames before individuals working at cross purposes are exposed.

At Chuck's company, previous managers had dropped the ball in two ways. First, they surrendered to a loopy notion rampant in the knowledge-worker arena today that all you have to do is hire the smartest people you can possibly find, and just get out of their way. In this particular case, the Decimalization Project (D Project) was largely dependent on large groups of young software programmers who, at the time this project was underway, were commanding six-figure salaries in their first few years out of college, despite having little maturity, business experience, or sense of accountability.

The hands-off attitude and the youth and inexperience of the workers led to the company's developing an immature, bifurcated culture. There were top managers who wanted only results and would just as soon not mingle with those curious youngsters with the tattoos and big clunky shoes. And there were talented, lower-level employees who didn't understand or care about the viability of the whole organization and their role within it. There were plenty of smart people in Chuck's company, but their managers got way too far out of their way. They stopped managing and started hoping and praying they'd hired people who "got it" and would deliver the goods.

Secondly and not surprisingly, because they stepped out of the way, the managers didn't impose a small handful of straightforward and fundamental points of discipline on knowledge work. They didn't assemble a clear list of programs and align them with their priorities; they didn't establish processes that could be cloned all over the company to dispatch D Project as efficiently as possible; and they didn't demand accountability. They allowed "stuff" to serve as the answer for what people were working on, and "in process" to substitute for a quantitative progress metric. The upshot was that management didn't know what people were working on, or how resources were actually being deployed. Middle-level managers were caught between trying to appease the top brass, and alienating the hard-working but independent and headstrong workers they needed to get the work done.

We were all too familiar with the nature of the workplace Chuck had walked into. Farzad and his brother Farid started a company called Diba with a team of hotshot computer guys, and they had the "hire-the-best-and-let-'em-rip" mentality. There is of course some truth in that sentiment. You can't hire very intelligent people and then micromanage them to the point where they can't relax and do their jobs. You can't fill their days with so much bureaucracy they can't be productive. But you also can't get sucked into thinking that because you paid top dollar for an employee, he or she knows best and so you'd better be prepared for surly grunts when you ask how things are going.

One reason the get-it cult tends to flourish in a knowledge workplace is that most CEOs hate to be bogged down in detail. And without a lot of hard metrics, the detail that attends knowledge-driven work tends to be very nuanced and complicated and difficult to interpret. A CEO's nightmare. Heaven for CEOs is a team of people who consistently provide concise, accurate information on which the CEOs can make decisions with high confidence. The more confidence a manager displays to his or her staff in relaying how things are going, the happier the staff.

That's when the mischief begins. Commonly, the first success was sheer luck or the kind of task about which the team is really excited and pumped up. Now, can the team repeat its success or deliver less glamorous work on time? The manager is basking in the warm, sunny glow of the CEO's affection from the first successful on-time, on-point delivery. A good manager is already developing an internal process for how the team delivered the first time and looking to further optimize it. The marginal manager is headed in the other direction: I've got a great team, I'm just going to step back and let them figure out what to do here, and I'll increase the reward if they repeat their success. Obviously, the team likes the second approach. But the signpost here should read: "The Road to Ruin."

Cutbacks and layoffs have put employers in the driver's seat again, and they have also focused managers' attention on the need to change the way they've been running knowledge workplaces, particularly services organizations. Many are being asked to change from being accounted for as a cost center to justifying their existence as a profit center. If they can't do it, they're gone. If employees won't get onboard and not only do the work but also provide managers with the information they need to monitor and account for resources on the projects, well, they'll be gone too.

Knowledge managers are desperate for help in making their knowledge workplaces more productive and their people more accountable. To help them, we've developed what we call the *Accountability Management System*—based on seven straightforward principles for managing a knowledge work or service organization. We believe these principles are bedrock ingredients for success.

On the basis of our customers' experiences and tracking against our own experiences, it's clear to us that a well-functioning workplace depends on three things that our system promotes: establishing a professional work culture with grownups in charge; following basic concepts regarding priorities, processes, and measuring progress; and always striving for transparency—or the ability of workers throughout the organization to understand its goals and priorities and where resources must be allocated.

Before we get into those tactics however, we want to say a few more words about some myths and realities that we perceive about knowledge workers today. You'll see why our system places so much importance on culture and the basic employer-employee contract. We believe that holding on to some of these myths gets in the way of effectively managing knowledge workers while missing opportunities that could arise from the positive attributes many of the knowledge workers bring to the business community.

Understanding Today's Knowledge Worker

In the last decade or so, the knowledge workplace has undergone dramatic change. New technology vastly increased the availability of information to workers of every sort, and the prolonged vibrant economy awakened and emboldened knowledge workers to demand more accountability from their own companies in order to win their loyalty or retain them as employees. Even though the stock market boom is over, we believe some of the workplace changes it set in motion have remained.

Reality 1. The younger knowledge workers (almost 40 percent of knowledge workers today are 34 or younger[5]) *are far more technology savvy and comfortable using and learning about new technology.*

The Nintendo generation is now in the workforce. They can hardly remember a time when e-mail wasn't available or cell phones weren't glued to everyone's ear. They've been typing on keyboards since preschool. Their idea of business dress may be khakis, a T-shirt, and tennis shoes, and tattoos may peek out from the sleeves of their shirts. But their technology savvy is an important development for the workforce. Consider how much time was spent in the 1980s trying to automate repetitive office tasks, "capture keystrokes," and streamline other ancient-sounding practices using technology. Think how many workers not only had to be educated about how to use computers but had to be convinced they were not evil or dangerous. Think of all the internal service time devoted to employees who simply refused to learn the most rudimentary aspects of their information technology. Young knowledge workers take technology for granted, as well as the notion that it is constantly being updated.

And that's just the generic worker. Also realize that advances in information technology have been invented and driven by young people. It's not for the students' sparkling conversation and fashion tips that so many venture capitalists prowl the halls of the computer science departments at Berkeley, Stanford, MIT, and other top schools. Those students are at the cutting edge of their fields. Yet for all the indulgences they enjoy in some organizations, in others the fundamental lack of respect for what they know is just as harmful.

Our friend Jeremy Wilkes is a management consultant and a former partner at Price Waterhouse Coopers, based in England. Wilkes has worked on engagements in which technically savvy younger workers were hired to implement strategy developed without their input—and the results were terrible. "The younger the person, the more realistic was their point of view because they knew the technology. They could say with a high degree of certainty what a realistic time schedule was," says Wilkes. "What happened was that these young peoples' opinions were delivered to middle management, managers who were clueless. Then, the senior people would make sweeping statements about what was and was not possible. . . . Everyone in the trenches understood the futility of the schedule. No one up above understood why things could not get done." What was lacking here, believes Wilkes, was "emotional insight," a form of transparency in which the groups looked past each others' ages and styles and had the appropriate level of respect for the other's knowledge base. These senior managers didn't want to know any technical details, and they didn't want to suffer through explanations. In fact, they ignored the junior technical peoples' forecasts and schedules.

Reality 2. As a group, today's knowledge workers are more ambitious at a younger age, they readily compare themselves to other knowledge superstars, and they are willing to work very hard.

Many workers today came of age during a period of unprecedented growth and change in the business world. More and more of them enjoy business, and they follow it the way some people follow sports. Attaining success and wealth is very high on their priority list, and their heroes are superstar entrepreneurs like Bill Gates, Larry Ellison, and Michael Dell, or Netscape's Marc Andreessen. This motivation and ambition, if properly channeled, can be enormously powerful for a company trying to compete in tough markets where speed is important. My friend Arnold Goto, a former partner at KPMG, turned this ambition into a recruiting tool. "In this job," he'd warn young recruits itching to get going, "you only have to work half days. Any 12 hours you want." It led to the "programmer-under-the-desk" mentality of the dot.com days where employees put in 20-hour marathon coding sessions and slept in the office.

Unfortunately, too many young employees today model themselves after the personalities of pathbreaking entrepreneurs. As successful as they are, would you want to run a company full of guys like Bill Gates or Larry Ellison? Probably not if your organization depends on teamwork and execution to deliver on its priorities and stay in sync. Teamwork can be undermined by unchecked ambition and drive in these younger individual team members. Even worse, some of these younger employees resent authority and monitoring. They chafe at being given direction, and they lack maturity in dealing with other members of a team. They may be smart, but in the context of a given organization, they may not work smart, often neglecting unglamorous but critical tasks in favor of chasing big ideas and trying to join initiatives they think are more exciting. Many of them never finish up and close the book on efforts that bore them. This type of knowledge worker must be given a crash course in Work 101.

Reality 3. Knowledge workers increasingly demand a big-picture understanding of the business and their place in it.

Twenty years ago, it was a rare entry-level worker who would study and personally evaluate the strategy of a potential employer. It was all about the job and the manager and the salary in the beginning. Companies felt no need to share higher-level insight with their lower-level employees—indeed, it was considered presumptuous to ask for it.

Today, new recruits come in armed for bear. If they can't connect the dots from their job to a financially sound, technically challenging strategic corporate initiative, they're not going to be interested. With a few taps on the keyboard and an Internet connection, they can gather all kinds of information about your company. Maddeningly, that information may come from wild-eyed, hysterical chatter on an investment bulletin board, as well as from objective, vetted commentary from respected sources. The recruits ask their hiring managers, and even the CEO, tough questions that would have truly been considered impertinent not too long ago. Sure, it's jarring to be a CEO doing a courtesy interview with a potential candidate for a lower-level job, and have that person start grilling you with the ferocity of a fund manager with millions of dollars of stock in your company. But as you will see, there are benefits to be had from transparency. We believe it can only help to have everyone in a company understand its strategy, goals, and priorities. And frankly, if you find yourself tempted to hide something from a young recruit, focus on fixing that problem, not on whether he or she should have asked the question.

However, transparency is not about a one-way information flow: "Your people need to understand the big picture and the overall budget," notes Jo Myland, a resource manager for Royal and Sun Alliance, one of the world's oldest insurance companies operating in 130 countries. Like us, Myland is a believer in time and progress tracking and other fundamental accountability principles. She wants something in return for the additional information she gives her people. "If they don't turn in their time cards, it impacts the company by preventing me from understanding and tracking their progress," she says. "If they understand the reason for what you want them to do, they are more likely to do it."

Reality 4. Knowledge workers want equity as well as salary, and they want to verify that they are making a good investment.

Employee equity is a double-edged sword. The use of options distributed even to low-level employees is designed to engender a sense of ownership in a business and to encourage employees to be willing to not only do their own job but to make sure they keep expenses in check and rectify mistakes quickly.

In the business world, we have just moved through an extraordinary period when making employees owners had a number of deleterious effects, however. Obsessively monitoring chat rooms about their own company's stock, swapping rumors with other employees, and checking the current stock price are all negatives. Another negative is the tendency of employees to become nervous and upset when the stock falls, even if the fall is related to broader market trends.

From a management point of view, you have got to focus on fundamentals. Don't confuse the stock price with the business—in either direction. Whether the company's stock is up or down, managers need to focus on the long-term success of the company, always keeping in mind that the day after a big surge or a fall, the company is the same company it was the day before, and it faces the same challenge: Execute on the plan.

That said, options are here to stay. Today's knowledge workers may be more interested in higher salaries and lower option packages than in the past, but that is an individual calculation each employee will make based on his or her own situation and faith in the company's business plan or strategy.

Reality 5. Knowledge workers have ready access to other opportunities and information about competitors, thanks to e-mail and the Web.

Any manager who thinks he or she is going to keep talented people indefinitely because the market has constricted is wrong. Comparing jobs, compensation, and benefits has become so much easier for employees. However, this is not something to fear. In Chapter 3, we'll discuss some very basic elements of inspiring and rewarding people. It's about a lot more than matching every salary offer.

The thing that ties these realities together for us is that they all relate to an exponential increase in employee exposure and access to information. Therefore, we tell managers to be as open as possible in making their priorities, goals, and plans public.

Openness is not, however, sufficient to mobilize a team. Unlike many managers of knowledge workers we've run across, we do not buy into much of the "new" thinking that the New Economy workplace is some kind of democratic idyll where knowledge is king, management is optional, and success is inevitable. Rather, we can't resist debunking what we believe are some myths about the knowledge work environment as well.

Five Dangerous Myths of the Knowledge Workplace

Myth 1. If you assemble a critical mass of very smart people, give them resources, and just leave them alone, great things will happen.

This is by far the most annoying and common misconception about managing knowledge workers that we hear. It is perpetuated by people who really don't know how to manage, by people so caught up in the need for speed that they feel they don't have time to manage. These managers perpetuate this swaggering mythology about management getting out of the way.

Of course you want to hire the best, the smartest people you can. When has that changed since the Stone Age? Who ever goes out and says: Find me someone really dumb to do this work? (Occasionally you might say, find me the best person you can for under $75,000 a year, but that is a different challenge.) The truth is that a roomful of smart people will not necessarily have a clue how to organize and manage themselves to success. In fact, the smarter they are, the more time they may spend fighting for dominance, back-biting, competing for attention, and ignoring directives from those they perceive as inferior. Those situations often are influenced by what we call "toxic knowledge workers," and we'll discuss them later in the book.

I love what Jeffrey Pfeffer, a professor at Stanford Business School, has to say about this. Pfeffer is coauthor of *The Knowing-Doing Gap*, which explores why, even when companies have best practices spelled out for them, so many just never embrace them to get the job done. He has said that one of the great myths of business in the 1990s was that the secret to success was just hiring great people. "Great companies are not built on great people," contends Pfeffer. "Great companies are built on systems that allow average people to deliver."

That resonates so strongly with us because we have never hired a person we didn't think was smart or capable. But we consider ourselves lucky if the majority of employees in our company get a C grade. Many CEOs boast that their teams are full of A players. Well, they may be full of people who have the potential to be A players, but they will never get an A from us unless they first complete all the tasks that we asked them to do, and then, and only then, can they go off and wow us with their creativity and drive on their own initiatives. We find that it's difficult to get everyone in the company just to complete baseline tasks. If you do those, you get a C. The Accountability Management System we're about to introduce you to is designed to emphasize full compliance on the business basics first. It is the kind of system we think Jeff Pfeffer had in mind.

Myth 2. You cannot hold knowledge workers accountable for their time, as they are creative and feel stifled by too much supervision.

Welcome to the real world. Assembly-line people feel stifled by too much supervision. CEOs feel stifled by too much supervision. NFL quarterbacks feel stifled by too much coaching. Salespeople feel stifled by too much supervision. What would happen if any of those groups were not held accountable for their time? What if a CEO had to report to the board only once a year? What if the quarterback woke up with a hangover on Super Bowl Sunday and asked for a one-week delay?

There is a world of difference between too much supervision and being held accountable for your time. The most basic contract we have when you work for us is that we pay you to work. If we didn't pay you, you wouldn't come to work. So, when you come to work, we have the right to see evidence of your work and progress. This does not mean we will sit in your cubicle and correct your posture while you're typing or that we will micromanage you, but we will expect you to be accountable for your time and progress. We will demand that specific and concrete milestones are met. The more consistently you meet those, the fewer there may be. However, without your appreciating that you must be accountable, we don't even have a conversation.

Myth 3. The work that most knowledge workers do is virtually unautomatable.

We agree that knowledge work is typically not about the repetition of identical tasks but about responding creatively and intelligently to some new proposition, reality, or challenge. The lore is that that response is best shaped by years of experience and handed down like tribal knowledge. That's why, for example, when Dave Raspallo, the EVP/CIO of Providence, Rhode Island–based Textron Financial, first broaches the subject of automation and process with groups under his direction, he says he hears a predictable litany of responses:

"If it ain't broke, don't fix it."
"I know how to do my job."
"I just know how to do it."
"This is simply bureaucracy."
"You want to do this just to protect your peoples' jobs."
"This is as good as it's going to get."

Raspallo doesn't buy it. Neither do we. Let's take a very creative endeavor to explain why. What is the exact method, for example, that a copywriter uses to come up with a spectacular advertising slogan? If we asked whoever wrote "Got Milk?" to write down the "steps," perhaps it would go: Discuss clients' goals with clients. Go to office. Stare out window for 2 hours. Play solitaire on computer for 1 hour. Suddenly snap to attention when slogan pops into mind. Write it down. Spend 2 days coming up with rationalizations for why it's perfect.

If we ask whoever came up with "Do you Yahoo?" for the creative system he or she used, it might well be: Assemble 20 copywriters in room. Fill up three whiteboards with ideas. Narrow down to five ideas. Show those to client who mentions she was thinking about "Do you Yahoo?" Throw out your ideas. Agree with client and compliment her for having the guts to suggest something you'd ruled out as too cutting edge earlier.

Is this evidence that you can't "automate" the creative process? Frankly, no. The discipline of project management allows a company to keep tabs even on creative efforts in such a way that managers know who is doing what, how they're spending their time, what their expected time to completion is, and what additional resources they need. That, in fact, is an automated process, in the sense that you can plan it in advance, anticipate progress, and use a software tool that helps you keep track of it all. The key is not to think of automation in terms of whether or not a computer could replace the person, but rather as a goal of accountability for a process that can and should be repeated consistently. Whether the idea pops into your head while jogging or sitting at your desk, you are accountable for making sure you had client input, you worked on this for a period of time when you were supposed to be working on it, you alerted management if you needed more resources to complete the activity, and you had the idea approved by the client.

Mature people understand this intuitively. Temperamental, erratic, immature workers probably also understand it, but they are wont to blame their environment, pressure from managers, bureaucracy, or distractions for why they haven't approached or delivered on an initiative in an accountable, responsible way. It's "the-dog-ate-my-homework" syndrome.

Myth 4. Your best workers need to be constantly stroked; be very, very afraid of losing them.

There are "franchise players" in every small company, and in many large ones, who are critical to the company's success. The best ones are so busy working, they are not difficult to manage. Others are prima donnas. We believe that no matter how high a pedestal you put an employee on, no matter how many unusual perks or personal valet services you offer, the main reason they will leave you is that the work they're doing is not interesting to them.

While it is important to let these individuals know you value them, we believe the old saying that everyone is replaceable. This goes back to some of the basic tenets of accountability: There is a hierarchy in this company. I may agree that you are outstanding and deserve vast riches and buckets of stock, but if you can't appreciate that you have a job to do, that you are accountable for your time and to a timeline, and that you must work on the mission-critical activities that management designates, then I wish you well in your next endeavor.

Myth 5. The company is the center of every young employee's life, and therefore the company should make sure that he or she is happy by keeping him or her amused and challenged.

We have grown to see that any company that takes on the role of cruise director and guidance counselor is asking for trouble. What's fun about work is doing it well and having it lead to success. Team building exercises and celebrations are morale-boosting events when they serve a purpose to the business. But just because you're asking employees to spend so much time in the office, you don't owe it to them to feed them, amuse them, entertain them, let them bring their dogs in, and teach their kids to ride a bicycle while their dad is away at a conference.

Except for brief, unavoidable spurts, marathon hours in the office aren't good for the company or the employees. Employees who are mature and have their own lives outside the office bring good judgment and perspective to work. The more the company becomes a refuge and an entertainment center, the more skewed the employees' perceptions are likely to become about their own value. And suddenly you have all kinds of petty venues where they compete and develop resentments. Who gets to be on the CEO's lunchtime roller hockey team? How come the foosball table in the R&D building is so much nicer than the one in finance? How can you tell me I need to be more efficient when I was here 80 hours last week? Encourage your employees to work smart and efficiently, get the hell out of the office at a reasonable time each night, and not come in on the weekends.

While all knowledge workplaces are subject to the pitfalls and challenges we have already discussed, the infusion of many younger, ambitious, tech-savvy young people has created an even more highly charged environment where patience and good judgment are not always in great supply, but where other benefits are emerging. We believe experience, or as we call it, adult supervision, is coming back in vogue. Many knowledge workplaces are energized and enhanced by the contributions of young knowledge workers, but the best are driven and led by experienced managers with the maturity to do what matters and to do it right, consistently. Now we'd like to discuss the principles the best of them tend to follow.

CHAPTER 2

Getting the Basics Straight
The Accountability Management System

What most people want is total freedom, no ground rules, and to be thought well of no matter what they do. Unfortunately, that is not going to work.

—MAYNARD WEBB
CHIEF OPERATIONS OFFICER OF EBAY

WE'VE COME UP WITH SEVEN BASIC PRINCIPLES that we use in managing our knowledge workplace and that we think you should use in managing yours. We distilled these rules from hours and hours of conversations with customers about what kinds of practices consistently produce the best results in the knowledge workplace. We reality-checked them against our own experiences and those of our friends and colleagues. They are very basic, not terribly clever-sounding ideas. No cheese was moved in the development of this system. But they speak to essential management attitudes and values.

We like to articulate them in a form that managers can use when speaking with their reports. Here goes:

1. Your job exists to make this company a success.
2. Yes, I am the boss of you.
3. The customer pays all of our salaries.
4. Do what matters.
5. Do it right.
6. Track your progress.
7. Work smart.

Rule 1. Your Job Exists to Make This Company a Success

Employees are paid for what they know and for what they can do for the company. The company compensates and rewards employees whose efforts make the company a success. The company doesn't seek to consume or replace employees' personal lives, complete their educations, expand their consciousness, help them achieve oneness, or nurture their inner child. Some or all of those things may happen anyway.

This rule is the *fundamental deal*. Unless your employees get this deal straight, all bets are off. Knowledge workers should understand and expect three things: They will get paid; they will be respected; and they will be given the appropriate tools to do their work. In return, they will do the work they're expected to do, respect the authority of the managers assigning the work, and contribute however they can to making the company succeed.

For many generations of workers, these truths were, to paraphrase the Declaration of Independence, "self-evident." But lots of well-intentioned but ineffective management styles have undermined workers' appreciation of the fundamental deal. For one thing, they have reinforced the notion among a certain percentage of workers that their employers owe them not only a paycheck but "happiness," whether in the form of games, outings, and social activities or in the kind of attention one might get from a school guidance counselor. The last situation is called the *mentor syndrome*, which is what our friend and former board member Maynard Webb so succinctly describes in the quote that leads off this chapter.

People are always telling college students and young people looking for a job that they should find a mentor. Movies and TV shows feature altruistic, kindly older gentlemen who take an interest in less experienced colleagues. They drink gin and tonics on the deck of the mentors' yacht. The mentors propel you straight to the top, love you no matter what, and ask for nothing in return. What a lovely idea. Sign me up!

There is, however, a different message that warrants equal time: Strive to be worth mentoring. The best and most valuable employees often display no sense of entitlement for mentoring. They will succeed with or without a mentor, and their work naturally gets them noticed and appreciated, and thus promoted. They don't waste any time looking at their bosses with a lopsided grin, admitting that they just weren't sure they knew what they really wanted to do or if they were happy. They recognize that their jobs exist so that they can deliver value to an enterprise that is trying to make money for its shareholders.

Does this sound harsh? Doesn't this fly in the face of "enlightened management" at companies that win all kinds of awards? No. We are not advocating mean, hard-hearted, nasty behavior. What we're talking about is a concept that respects the fundamental maturity of every individual employee. Do you know why you're here? You are here to add value to the company. You are here to do an important job. You are here to use your exceptional knowledge and apply it to complex situations. You will be challenged, and you will be tested. We hope you succeed. We need you to succeed in order for the company to succeed.

If you don't have the fundamental premise straight, nothing else we're about to suggest to you is likely to work. Our Accountability Management System is based on some very old-fashioned and time-tested values such as hierarchy, personal responsibility, attention to customer needs, and activity management techniques. All these components demand accountability to the people paying your salary. If you aren't willing to enforce a grown-up culture in which people leave the *in loco parentis* days of college behind, good luck getting the employees to account for their time, share their knowledge, and perform constant goal and alignment checks, as well as working through some of the other activities that are vital for success.

Rule 2. Yes, I Am the Boss of You

There is a hierarchy in this company. Managers have the blessing and support of the CEO to make decisions, and, in turn, the responsibility to maximize the talent resources they are given. Working smart is more important than being smart. *Working smart* means completing high-priority assignments before doing anything else. The company supports an open and vigorous debate until a decision is made—and then all hands are on the oars.

Life is often fuzzy in knowledge organizations partly because there are many ways to do just about everything. To encourage people to come forward with good ideas and to enhance communication, some managers mistakenly try to create a flat structure and minimize and downplay hierarchy. They play up the "we're one big happy family of smart people" mantra. In the process, they unwittingly encourage people to go behind each others' backs to lobby and backstab, to sneak off and work on unauthorized but more appealing work, or to try to read tea leaves about which executive has the CEO's ear in order to align with the "winning team." This wastes time, brainpower, and talent.

Hierarchy is very, very important. We don't mean oppressive, military-style hierarchy. Hierarchy does not mean master-slave relationships. As a manager, you should always pay close attention to your managers' ability to use their peoples' knowledge to the fullest. It's their job to maximize the talent at their disposal, and deploy it in a way that motivates the employees to succeed. You want your managers to listen. You want them to hire smart people who can advance so that you will never have to hear an employee defended with the assertion, "Well, he's not very good, but if we didn't have him we'd have nothing."

However, you should have a strict rule in managing your people: If your employees work for you, then that means you believe they are smart and capable of doing their job. They are the de facto standard for their position. If the organization did not have faith in them, they would not be here. Therefore, if there is a question about how your group should do something, you, the manager, will decide. Your boss will live with your decision, you will live with it, and they will live with it. They will add as much value as possible to the activities as the decision demands. If they attempt to undermine the decision, they will face severe consequences.

This rule does not necessarily limit people. Knowledge workers are free to suggest and pursue other opportunities, for example, as long as they get their own chores done first. If the knowledge worker is ambitious and creates new opportunities in addition to performing assigned duties, he or she will thrive in a hierarchical organization as well. That individual will make his or her boss happy and also look good by delivering the goods. Then comes the opportunity to wow his or her own boss or other senior managers with creative, perhaps nonlinear thinking or ideas. Don't be boxed by your manager's box is one of our rules. Once you've delivered on the priorities your manager has requested, go ahead and try to conquer the rest of the world.

The crux of enforcing our form of hierarchy is not harboring any "dead men walking." You know what we're talking about—the people in an organization who are being slowly, excruciatingly pushed out. Everyone knows they are on their way out; everyone knows they are lame ducks; everyone knows they have lost all power. Until they finally leave, they are the people about whom other employees whisper: "She must have pictures of the CEO with a farm animal."

Everyone in your organization should be presumed competent. If you have concerns about an individual, you should watch the person very carefully, trying to help if you can, but once you decide the individual is not, in fact, best for the job, you should move that person out. Failing to act quickly in these cases is what we call "playing with the snake." If you pick something up and it turns out to be a snake, what do you do? Anyone who is not a member of a fundamentalist sect in the Ozarks throws it down. Once you realize something is a snake, get rid of it, or it will bite you.

Rule 3. The Customer Pays All of Our Salaries

Knowledge workers and internal service providers need to be just as focused on improving efficiency, quality, and service to customers as anyone else in the company. Every initiative aimed at increasing revenues or reducing expenses should be considered in light of its impact on customers first.

You occasionally visit companies whose lunchrooms or cubicle walls are filled with inspirational posters about the importance of customers. But when you walk around inside some of those same companies' service groups, you'll hear people talk as if the customers are the enemy— a target to be cajoled, manipulated, appeased, bamboozled, put off, stalled, or convinced that they don't want what they want. At Oracle, Farzad had a manager who once opened a meeting about trying to help a customer who was struggling with an installation of Oracle software with these inspiring words: "Rule 1, the customer is always stupid."

We encourage employees to draw a direct line between their job and a paying customer. Then, they need to conduct themselves in a way that shows respect and attention to customer needs. One interesting thing about knowledge workers and customers: The negative impact of a knowledge worker's offending or disappointing a customer or making a mistake is often disproportionate to that individual's role in the organization. A customer service representative who botches a service call, for example, can undermine an enormous investment of time and resources the sales team and executives have made in winning that business. A cavalier or ignorant performance by a business development person can destroy a chance for a critically needed deal. When your currency is information, credibility and integrity are easily eroded by arrogance or carelessness.

When you're tucked into the middle of a service group inside a company, it's very easy to lose sight of bill-paying customers. Internal service providers come to think of their managers and executives as their customers. There is a tendency to think of executives as the "big" customers, regardless of the merits of a request or where it falls on the priority list. And it's always hard to say no to a big customer. This is why some of the other "sins" of our system, such as executives interrupting work and managers failing to broadcast a clear sense of priorities, are so debilitating.

Managers all the way up the chain, and certainly including the CEO, need to recognize the big internal customer problem. Here's an example: We were recently presented with a requisition for doing a Japanese translation of our product. It would have cost us $150,000, and it was ordered by a development manager because one prospective customer said his organization would need this capability before it would sign a deal to buy our software.

Unraveling this mess—it turned out the prospect had already agreed to purchase the software without a Japanese translation—led us straight to Farzad's door. In trying to communicate to our development group that he wanted them to be very sales and customer focused, Farzad used the expression "do whatever it takes" to equip our sales force to sell the product. When the salespeople asked the head of development if they could do the translation, he aligned with what he thought were the wishes of his biggest customer (Farzad), never taking into account that, given the size of this deal, spending another $150,000 on a Japanese translation would not have made any fiscal sense. He overvalued his internal customer's vague directive over the reality of the relationship with a real customer. In turn, Farzad's comments were too big and sweeping. It's a much longer walk from an employee's office to the CEO's to ask for clarification and the parameters than it is from the CEO's office to the employee's to make sure the employee understands how to implement a new initiative.

Rule 4. Do What Matters

No company can do everything. Management has to establish and broadcast priorities for the company and then support those priorities by not interrupting mission-critical activities with low-priority work. Management must also reward individual contributors for completing important targets first, before advancing new ideas or pursuing low-priority endeavors.

Once an organization grows beyond a very small number of people, setting and broadcasting priorities is the bedrock component of the tactical steps of accountability management. Ask: What matters to this company? What matters most to this company? Of the things that matter most to the company, which are we pursuing in an optimal way?

We recently met with the executive in charge of a $120 million R&D organization in the drug industry. In discussing our product, we mentioned that many customers come to us because they realize their organizations have grown beyond their own understanding. They literally can't account for large portions of their budget or for what their people are working on.

It happened that this executive had brought a lower-level manager into the meeting, and he ran about $75 million worth of the $120 million budget. "Oh, I know what my people are doing. I know how this money is being spent," the other manager said. "But the other $45 million is kind of questionable. We're not really sure where all that is going." The higher level manager nodded, but he considered it acceptable that he at least knew what was going on in more than half his organization. Think of the waste and inefficiency this kind of complacency suggests.

The goal is to create a culture in which every single employee is constantly performing an alignment check between individual efforts and decisions, and with what matters most to the company's survival and/or success. Knowledge workers without direction may understandably be tempted to do all kinds of things at odds with what the company needs—activities that satisfy their curiosity or personal career interests; activities a high-level executive requests as a favor (and please note, that person also does not have the deal straight if he or she interrupts more important work to ask that favor); tasks that are easy, as opposed to hard; initiatives that are interesting, as opposed to dull. None of these are criminal acts. They are the acts of people who are not being properly managed. Matching up the work with the people who will be intrigued and engaged and motivated to do a good job with it is all part of the art of being a good manager. However, the organization's priorities rule the day. In Chapter 5, we will elaborate on the process of managing a work portfolio by first aligning initiatives with corporate priorities, and we will explore the important cultural elements of ensuring that those priorities are made clear, are broadcast, and are reality-checked.

Rule 5. Do It Right

Processes are not a bureaucratic luxury. They are critical to a well-functioning, efficient knowledge workplace. Every knowledge activity requires that sequential steps be taken and that efforts be coordinated. Management will require rigorous, structured knowledge-work management discipline; however, it will encourage employees to own and constantly improve the processes of their actual work.

Respect for process was one of the biggest casualties of the New Economy boom. The fallout has ranged from failure to elaborate frauds. A recent SEC filing showed, for example, that Adelphia Communications, Inc., is fighting for its life now after allegations that the company paid hundreds of millions of dollars to members of the majority-owning family to cover margin calls, condos, and—our personal favorite—a $1.3 million annual salary to a son-in-law of the founder, who ran a venture capital firm that had made only $1 million in actual investments. An outside board has now taken over the company to try to stave off bankruptcy. They're a little late to the party. Adelphia is a publicly traded company, and as such, it should have had corporate governance processes in place that would have bounced those transactions sky high. Instead, we're sure the board was told "trust us, we get it." Boy, did they get it.[1]

More commonly, roving bands of knowledge workers with toxic tendencies mock or ignore process in the workplace, calling it "bureaucracy." But you don't "just do it." You must do it right, and do it repeatedly, and do it in such a way that it can be tracked and taught, and corrected, if need be. Following accepted processes is an essential element in accountability management. In Chapter 6, Rhonda will discuss in some detail the two key processes companies must embrace in order to establish an accountable culture.

Rule 6. Track Your Progress

A company must utilize time and progress tracking to improve its total visibility and flexibility in the context of a dynamic and challenging business environment. The company can't assess and improve upon what it can't measure.

Knowledge workers tend to cast everything they do in the realm of quality, not quantity. Of course, one can't measure the true value of an attorney, for example, by the sheer number of contracts he or she reviews in a given week; one can't value a public relations person on the number of embarrassing or negative stories that *didn't* appear in the press in a given week. But once we adopt a progress-oriented approach to managing initiatives within the company, milestones are created that do, in fact, represent a method for measuring whether the activity is moving along as expected, at a reasonable cost, and with desirable results.

The three P's—prioritize, process, and progress tracking—become a closed-loop, self-reinforcing system for keeping things on track. Problems in one area will be outed by another. Progress tracking can reveal whether flaws in process are unduly holding up progress on corporate priorities. Process adjustments can help an activity from veering off course from high-priority to marginally valuable activities. Put all these elements in place, and soon you can answer an essential question for any manager: Are we doing what matters effectively and in a timely manner?

Rule 7. Work Smart

Seek knowledge. Share knowledge. The company must embrace tools that foster maximum visibility and transparency of operations.

There is no question that for two decades "knowledge management" systems have foundered. The early promise of artificial intelligence and exaggerated "office automation" schemes became a cloud over the whole idea. But such basic productivity tools as e-mail and intranets are driving the ability of companies to respond faster and in more organized ways to myriad new challenges. The problem, however, is that without the right cultural underpinnings, the new tools are unproductive. If an appreciation for the top six rules does not exist, new information technologies can't improve efficiency in the knowledge workplace because the people using them aren't bringing a dedicated heart and mind to the effort. The elements of our Accountability Management System all build upon the previous step, and you need everything right in order to best take advantage of new knowledge tools, which we'll discuss in Chapter 10.

Those are the nuts and bolts of our system. Are you running a mature, accountable organization that is delivering ever-increasing value? Or do you feel like Chuck from the last chapter, struggling to get a handle on what people are doing and whether they'll get what you need done on time? Ideally, you'll follow these ideas and come to feel more like Maynard Webb, whose observations led off this chapter.

Maynard's experience at eBay could have turned him into Son of Chuck. Instead, eBay is now commonly regarded as the dot.com that could, a rare example of a success story on an otherwise bleak landscape. Maynard's contribution to that was huge. He joined the company in 1999, a rough time in eBay's history, when the company was getting front-page and nightly news treatment for its less than reliable Web site.

It was crucial for eBay to restore reliability to its system, despite the incredible growth the IT organization was being asked to support. Maynard had come from Gateway, where he had been chief information officer and senior vice president. Maynard recalls that when he arrived at eBay, his people were confused about who was doing what and what needed to be done. They had become somewhat addicted to living on the edge. When something happened right, it always seemed to be the result of Herculean effort.

Today, however, Maynard's organization is delivering six times more work than it did before he took over. They have increased their capacity to handle unscheduled work by 20 percent. And, their on-time delivery percentage is 90 percent. System availability is over 99.9 percent.

How did he get them there? By using common sense, maturity, and accountability management.

The first thing he did was set expectations and make sure people got the deal straight about working for him: "You need to spend your time making sure all your people understand where they are supposed to go and make sure that they are spending all of their energies getting there." Maynard also understands that he doesn't employ robots. Good knowledge workers need a good challenge, and he points out problems to them and dares them to solve them on a daily basis. He says, "Any world-class department will eventually figure out how to make the critical path something other than themselves."

He demands weekly accountability to schedules and game plans. And in those sessions, he welcomes discussion of problems. He just wants to make sure the team flags them early so that they can do something about it.

He also implemented several changes to the business in order to achieve more customer focus. As manager of an IT organization, he was one degree of separation away from the customer. He knew that in order to be successful, he needed to partner with the business units to meet the customers' needs. So he took the radical step of requiring a commitment on the business units' side as well. Everyone at eBay needs to present to Maynard his or her business case before Maynard commits his organization's resources. This had the effect of focusing both organizations' attention on the customer and forcing them to really think about and understand what the customer would want. He thinks this has increased the quality of the requirements that he gets. He also set up schedules for formal processes to make sure that his customers receive the business benefits they expect.

"Things that last hundreds of years can't be based on the heroics of individuals," notes Maynard. "Brilliance is much rarer than people think. I'd much rather push process, systems, and repeatable stuff. If you give enough credit to folks who are doing these jobs but also force them to look in the mirror and be accountable, good things will happen."

Here's a quick assessment you can make of your own workplace:

1. The basic deal
   - Do your employees understand why they're working here and what you're paying them for?
   - Do they understand that their success is dependent upon the company's success?
2. The hierarchy
   - Do your employees understand the importance of hierarchy in a functioning workplace? Do they accept the priorities their manager sets?
   - Do they accept that sometimes knowledge work is not black and white but the manager is still responsible for setting direction?
   - Do they understand their place in the organization? Do they understand their primary responsibilities?
3. The customers
   - Do your employees have a good sense of the company's customers and what their needs are?
   - Do they understand the difference between a real, live, paying customer and management?
   - Do they realize that customer input is more important than their opinion?
4. Doing what matters
   - Do your employees know which activities to work on?
   - Do they understand the company's strategic direction?
   - Do they understand the part they play in implementing this direction?
5. Doing it right
   - Do your employees feel that they're working for an efficient organization?
   - What kind of help or support for changes would help them?
   - Can they explain, step by step, how they perform important, repeated tasks?
   - Do they understand best practices for their activities?

6. Tracking progress
   - Do your employees understand the importance of providing you with consistent information regarding the progress of their work?
   - Can they estimate the amount of time it will take them to perform critical tasks?
   - Do they communicate problems with the planned completion date of any activity?
7. Working smart
   - Do your employees know what types of information would help them do their job better?
   - Do they realize the importance of sharing information and experiences or are they knowledge misers?

Inspiring and Rewarding Employees

Y OU CAN'T LEGISLATE CULTURE. You can't dictate attitude. You can't mandate maturity.

However, the first three principles of accountability management—
getting the basic deal straight, establishing and enforcing the hierarchy,
and respecting the customers—are all about culture. If your organization
falls down in one or more of those areas, your employees will not be prepared to conduct themselves in an accountable way. So, if you can't legislate, mandate, or dictate culture, how do you fix things?

You lead. You set an example. You be the grown-up. You keep an eye
out for signs that you or somebody else has cultivated unproductive and
even destructive behaviors in your workplace. And you learn to motivate your employees in a way that speaks to their value, integrity, and
maturity.

So many of the things that frustrate managers have their roots in
misguided efforts to motivate people. Managers want their people to do
well, to deliver heroics, to perform miracles. What they don't understand is that well-run organizations can do extremely well without
heroics and miracles. As Maynard Webb once put it: "We had to get rid
of the idea that it was cool to live on the edge."

Harry Truman said something we love: The world is run by C students. Lots of managers—CEOs and team leaders alike—swagger
around claiming that they can do what they do because they hire only
world-class people with world-class skills who do world-class work.

That's pep rally talk. We are thrilled if we feel our workforce has a typical bell curve made up mostly of C students.

To get a C, your employees have to do what you tell them to do. That's your baseline. The problem with young hotshots is that they want to run off and do what they want to do, and they think you'll be so appreciative you'll let them off the hook for their assigned—probably boring—work. Don't. The cost of getting to the higher-level dance is paying their admission with their assigned work. If they do that, then they can go off and wow you with their new ideas and proposals.

If managers deliver on their part of the equation and make sure the troops deliver all the assigned, boring work, they're usually way ahead of the game. But that's not what happens. Managers get distracted with pet projects or they are intimidated by the demands or tantrums of certain workers or teams. They perceive things starting to run amok, then they panic and turn up the heat on the presumed superstars while neglecting the others.

Weird things start to happen in the culture when management goes into a panic and the "pay no attention to the man behind the curtain" mode. You get elaborate loyalty displays, for example. Employees begin performance reviews talking about the amount of stock they have purchased and how many Saturdays they've worked. Teams develop a seething hatred of other teams, and they plot to blame these other teams for all delays and setbacks. Water-cooler chatter is about the pharmacy of flu palliatives on the desk of someone who is working despite a 102° fever. Caricatures of customers considered to be difficult appear on the lunchroom bulletin board, and eventually the eyeballs are gouged out.

Then, there are individual acts of rebellion. Senior-level executives find themselves blind-cc'ed on messages clearly designed to "expose" the faulty thinking of a lower-level manager. Or employees set up internal debit and credit ledgers, where they keep track of every perceived plum or reprimand and are constantly pointing out injustices—à la the dysfunctional family Christmas when the kids tally up the value of the gifts and proclaim a winner and loser.

The way to look at it is not all that different from the way parents would look at a parallel situation. We don't mean this in a condescending way, and we realize there are limits to the analogy. However, managers need to spend time with their employees, understanding what they're doing, communicating their expectations, and keeping them accountable—just as parents need to spend time with their children.

Farzad worked directly for Larry Ellison for 3 years. Given Ellison's reputation as a billionaire playboy with a stable of jets and a penchant for death-defying yacht races, the words "maturity and common sense" may not immediately spring to mind at the sound of his name. But Ellison became a billionaire, and Oracle has thrived and grown because he hired smart people, and he got them to work their tails off. How did he do this?

Not by leaving a briefcase of cash on his reports' desks. He did it by being very smart and appreciating the input of smart people—in fact, appreciating it to the extent that he will give you something very valuable if you can prove yourself to him: time. Ellison pays attention to the people working for him. He calls them on the carpet if they screw up. He respects them if they bring home the product or the deal. He makes his managers ride their people and stay on top of their programs and spend time with their people. His wrath is like frontier justice: swift and severe. From time to time he goes AWOL with some regatta or other interest, and when he does that, things inside Oracle go off course too. But when he gets back to work, Oracle has traditionally gotten back on track. That's not a fluke.

In a more familiar example, consider the famous "HP Way," which is now said to be up for grabs in the wake of the HP-Compaq merger. Whether the legacy of Bill Hewlett and Dave Packard is still viable or not, for decades that company was run on the basis of management's paying close attention to the people who worked for them. Hewlett and Packard walked around the company, and they encouraged people to come to them and discuss what was going on.

There is also what we call the *Fonzarelli Factor* at work here. After all these years of seeing Oracle through good times and turning it around when it went off track, Ellison has credibility with his people. His people know deep down that he can manage better than they can. He's been there, he's done that. Similarly, guys like Hewlett and Packard had tremendous credibility with their engineers. They were engineers, and employees always believed that getting their hands dirty and building great products was their favorite part of the job. Successful managers must be able to project their experience to their people, or the employees just won't perform for them.

We would love to tell you the Fonzarelli reference is to some Italian political genius from the fourth century, or at least to some management scholar whose research is regularly referenced in the *Harvard Business Review*. In fact, we're talking about "The Fonz," the character Henry Winkler played in the old *Happy Days* television show. When Farzad first arrived in the United States from Iran in the late 1970s, he used to gorge on cheesy American TV show reruns. His Fonzarelli Factor refers to how The Fonz was about 5 feet, 2 inches tall, but he never had to swing an arm because his reputation for toughness preceded him. Pure intimidation.

It's human nature to look for shortcuts or gimmicks and tell yourself you don't have time to do exactly the thing that you should do because it is hard work. It's easier to buy the toy and spoil the kid than take the time to talk to the kid about why temper tantrums are unacceptable.

We speak from experience. As you'll see in Chapter 9, we've paid the bills for Nerf guns. We've dodged programmers who've set up elaborate steeplechases through the hallways when they're supposed to be working. We've tried lionizing developers to the point where they expected an engraved invitation and a limousine to attend a meeting.

One thing we haven't tended to do because we know it has never worked is write checks to get people to improve their performance. Check writing, however, was rampant in other companies during the dot.com explosion. But it didn't help. It just doesn't work to throw money at people to buy their hearts. In fact, financial incentives have a 48-hour lifespan. When you are trying to get somebody to focus heart and mind on the challenge at hand or you are trying to keep someone from leaving, a financial lollipop will cheer them up in the short term but the effect won't last. If the person has a fundamental problem with his or her job or with his or her manager, the money will only delay the inevitable. In fact, it often makes the employee even more cynical. The best motivator is cool stuff to work on for somebody who knows good work when he or she sees it.

None of that should be construed to read that you shouldn't pay people well, that you should not give bonuses or rewards for a job well done. You should. But what about the scenario in which somebody approaches his or her manager and says he or she is going to take another job because it pays 30 percent more, at which point his or her manager begins scrambling, and, within a day or two, finds the money to match the increase. What has happened here?

Well, one thing that's probably happened is that the manager has been trying to take some of the credit that the employee deserves. The manager has failed in a key way: He or she hasn't been selling the employee's talents. When that employee threatens to leave, the manager panics and realizes he or she can't keep up the performance illusion without the key employee onboard. So the manager scrambles to give the rewards and recognition the employee should have been given long ago.

You should give people financial bonuses or options awards because you have observed them doing a good job and you want them to *stay* happy. Avoid the fire drills created by postponing the rewarding of good people until they become angry and demand it.

Recognition is more important to employees than financial incentives. With this in mind, you should identify the people in the organization who have promise and then pay attention to them. Talk to them. Talk to other people about them. Encourage your reports to sell their employees to you. You don't want the first time you hear about somebody who wants or needs a raise to be the day he or she wants or needs the raise. Managers should be encouraged to be actively promoting their own people all the time because that builds loyalty and makes the company more confident in their management abilities as well.

In the last chapter, we gave you a concise list of things to think about in assessing your organization. If you're not thrilled with the answers you came up with to those questions, let's talk about how you can move your organization in the right direction in the context of the first three rules of accountability management. If you feel it's time to hit the reset button, you've got to start investing some time in this. Start with a one-on-one conversation with the people who report to you. The conversation is the same for a CEO and his or her direct reports as it is for a project manager and his or her team members. It involves three basic operating principles we introduced in the last chapter, all of which speak to the attitude and professionalism of the workplace.

1. The Basic Deal

We'll start with the fundamental deal: Do your people understand why they're working here and what you're paying them to do?

Fixing a corporate culture that's out of whack means going back to the basic proposition, the fundamental assumptions of employment. The question above is partly about attitude and willingness to work and partly about identifying "manageable" employees and employees who need to either shape up, grow up, or find a new crib.

Every now and then in every important relationship, it helps to make sure we share the same assumptions and that our heads are screwed on straight about what we're doing. Asking someone why she's working at your company and what she's being paid to do has an astounding and powerful effect on the employee. Think about the people who report to you, and imagine sitting them down, one by one, and asking them this question. How will each respond? What is the ideal answer you'd like to hear from each? If you're feeling extremely brave and have a few free hours to develop your own answers (and handle the fallout), you can even practice this on your spouse or significant other. "What are we doing in this relationship, and what do you feel you are contributing to it?"

If you invite your reports to sit down with you and you ask them this question, odds are that your best workers will visibly pale and start sweating. Your mediocre to minimal contributors will look at you incredulously, as if to say, "If you have to ask, why are you my boss?" That's because your best people probably are asking themselves this all the time, wisely trying to adjust their performance to the needs of the organization, and they are feeling a little paranoid that they're not doing it well enough. The low-value people, meanwhile, have constructed an elaborate internal monologue that everyone is out of step but them.

But anyway, try this. Ask them directly: Why are you here, and what is it you are being paid to do?

You cannot anticipate all the specific things your people will tell you, but when you've done this, you'll come away with incredibly useful information that you couldn't have gleaned any other way. Typically, your faith will be simply restored in good, smart workers. They may be very specific about what they're doing—and they're correct in that specificity. Or they may be more global and give you an answer like: "I am here to provide as much value as I can to make this company succeed."

These folks can nonetheless help expose specific areas where your communication may have been poor. You will be surprised at how they may very readily take the opportunity to say: "You know, I've been thinking it's top priority for me to deliver X, but I wonder if my priorities are correct given that Y has happened." You, as their manager, may never have drawn a connection between those events. You can now see how others may have done that, and you can address that more broadly.

Another category of workers to whom you ask this question will come away truly enlightened and change behavior based on their new understanding. There are people, some very talented, others marginal, who go off track. Neither they nor even you may have even realized it has happened. They are not dumb or belligerent, but they are typically reluctant to stick their heads above the bunker and admit they aren't exactly sure what's going on or how they're supposed to be contributing at this juncture. Many of these people got a C in math in high school because they were too embarrassed to ask the same question that the A students queried the teacher about after class was over.

It is very important with these people (really with everyone in this exercise) to ask these questions in a neutral, curious way, not in the tone of voice you take with your kids when you say "HEY, did you hear what I just SAID? What do you think you're DOING?" Tell them you're doing a reality check and making sure corporate priorities and style are being communicated properly. Then listen carefully to what they say.

The third category of workers will break your heart. You may discover workers who not only do not understand what they specifically are supposed to be doing but who truly do not understand the entire proposition of working here. They may have mentor syndrome, and they will literally use the question as an excuse to riff on their needs or wants. "I've been wondering that myself," they might answer. "I'm just not sure I'm challenged with the [insert project] I've been working on." Or they may have that one-big-happy-family problem and answer cheerfully, "I'm here to have fun." Or "I'm here to raise enough money so I can quit working and finance my Olympic dreams." Or they may give you a specific answer so off base from what you really want them to be doing that you will instantly come to some new realization about them—you might need to put them on probation, move them to a new position, or simply get them out of your organization.

2. The Hierarchy

The second question you're going to ask your people is how they feel about the priorities that you have articulated to them. Do they agree with those priorities? How do they intend to meet them? Do they accept your authority to communicate these priorities?

This conversation is as much a reminder to them as it is an investigation for you. If an employee admits he or she does not accept your authority, you should suggest that he or she either learn to do so or find a new position. It's as simple as that. There is a hierarchy in this company because it is essential for productivity and efficient decision making.

Workers are always free to suggest ways the company can help them be more efficient or productive. However, workers may not work around you to get their way. They may not use the bcc function in their e-mail program to embarrass, expose, torpedo, or attack a manager or a colleague.

Also, ask them if they think that you listen to them. Ask them if they're getting the things they need in order to be successful. You may get a wish list of everything from free lattes to a masseuse that comes in on Tuesdays between 11:30 and 12:30. You'll probably also be asked for clearer direction, better tools, and more feedback. You can deal with these requests as you see fit. But the fact that you're asking will probably, in and of itself, go a long way to filling some existing felt needs.

There are times when the hierarchy must be enforced in a brutally honest way. Our favorite example is what we call the "Big Guy" story from British-based Marlborough Stirling, a leading provider of customized software and services to the lending and investment markets. David Phillips, corporate services and financial director, was telling Rhonda his take on the role of adult supervision. One of his organization's workers, a beefy soccer fanatic, asked his manager for the day off so he could attend a football match. The manager said he couldn't give it to him, as a particularly crucial project was nearing the final stretch. The next time the Big Guy's team had a match, the Big Guy simply called in sick.

Phillips asked the manager to have the Big Guy come see him for a meeting. He let the Big Guy cool his heels a bit, and then he burst into the room with a big smile. "I want to shake your hand," Phillips told him as the puzzled Big Guy grasped his outstretched paw. "You've proved me right. I told your manager when you were hired that you were lazy, and you are."

The Big Guy broke into tears. Phillips told him, "It's your choice, work or go home." The Big Guy chose the former. He stopped calling in sick, and he became a good worker. Phillips said he never brought it up again, in fact, and, he would joke with the Big Guy in the hallways later, signaling that the episode was forgotten. Be honest with people. It saves time.

3. The Customers

Ask your reports: Who is your customer? What are his or her needs? What are you doing to fill those needs? How is whatever it is you're doing taking the customer's needs into account?

As we have already mentioned, a recurring problem in the knowledge workplace is that when the needs of bill-paying customers are not made explicit to an organization, even very good workers have a tendency to regard internal customers—namely, top executives—as their true customers. Salespeople have a very clear idea of whom they need to please to make their numbers—the customers who buy the products. But knowledge workers often limit their own effectiveness to the larger organization by narrowing their focus. When we see evidence of this, we pull an employee aside and say, "Don't be boxed by your manager's box."

There are two components to this box that are important. The first is that we don't want employees to define their scope and thinking at the company as concerning only those things for which their manager has responsibility. Smart people who are alert to the true needs and pains of customers are a huge asset to a company. We can't afford to let a manager confine his or her employees' thinking to the manager's zone alone. That's one reason we not only allow but encourage intracompany transfers. Slavery was abolished long ago. Employees who demonstrate that they can be just as productive or more productive somewhere else in the company where they will also be happier have our blessing to change jobs. In fact, we put the blame on an employee's existing organization for not managing the person well enough that the individual wants to stay, rather than creating high hurdles for the new manager to argue that he or she should be allowed to hire the employee.

Some companies actually create the problem of internal customer confusion on purpose by launching their own internal service or component companies that bill their products or services to other departments. Information technology groups have a terrible time with this. Some IT groups have no understanding of who their ultimate customer is. These corporate divisions are instead forced to deal with business lines who filter customers' requests and who then complain that IT doesn't understand the business they are in. Well-run organizations have a well-aligned IT group that works in concert with the business lines, as partners, to deliver something to the customer. It could be a Web-based order tracking system or a consolidated billing statement. An IT organization that works with customers is better able to deliver value to customers.

There is a potential to capture considerable yet unpredictable value by simply having smart people throughout a company buying into the idea that the customer pays the bills and the customer's needs are paramount. There was a period when Farzad worked at Oracle when the company didn't really realize the degree to which their customers were using Oracle's software to actually run their businesses. At one point, Oracle had a big customer in Australia whose system went down. Oracle's relationship to this customer was so distant, both literally and figuratively, that it took 4 or 5 days just for the customer to get a response from Oracle, and it took something like 2 weeks more for Oracle to actually address the problem. The customer had to shut down its operations for 2 weeks while Oracle fiddled around, costing the customer millions in revenues. Perversely, the customer had to teach Oracle how important Oracle could be to a large operation.

We guarantee this interview exercise is going to give you new insights into the people working for you. You may not love some of the insights you get, but you will be a better manager for not ducking these basics. Revving up the power and efficiency of your organization is going to work only if you're dealing with adults who have a mature attitude about their role in the organization. All the excuses they may attempt to give you later on for why they don't want to change the way they've been doing things, or why they don't think it's "fair" that you want to measure and track their progress, or why they don't want you to manage their projects in a consistent, rigorous way can typically be answered by referring back to these three principles.

It's worth keeping these elements in mind when interviewing new candidates for a job as well. You have no history with them yet, so paying close attention to their willingness to be accountable to a hierarchy and to really serve customers will help you work with them down the road.

Knowledge Worker Archetypes

Once you do these interviews, odds are your people will start to gel into certain types of recognizable personalities for you. At one level is the report card–style classification system of A, B, C, D, and Forget-it workers. At another level, however, are functional archetypes. You name a profession or an industry and its members probably can outline for you the basic personality types of those who populate it. If you say somebody is a "sales type," that brings certain traits to mind immediately, such as aggressive, personable, driven, and competitive. In fact, some-one who doesn't have some of those traits is unlikely to be much of a salesperson.

The "typical" knowledge worker is a complex character. Accountants, tech support folks, marketing managers, attorneys—each group has its own subgroups and personality types. You could spend the rest of your life becoming a Ph.D. in the nuances of these personalities. Don't do that. But there are some common characters in the knowledge workplace who pose management challenges. Do invest some time in learning the differences between the types of behaviors you can work with and those that can really sap the life out of your organization.

The Fixable Knowledge Workers

The Jock

This worker wants to "just do it." Hates process and bureaucracy, values independence. Likes to work alone. Unfortunately, often goes off half-cocked in the wrong direction. Has "Ask forgiveness, not permission" sign hung over desk. Has to ask for a lot of forgiveness, as he or she gets miles off track before he or she knows he or she is lost. Never reads the agenda before the meeting, never asks directions.

These folks are a management challenge, but they tend to have good morale and lots of energy. And they can be extremely productive if you put them on a pedestal for things they're good at. Keep a close watch over them, but don't put them in a position of authority until they grow up. They must learn to consistently ask for and welcome feedback, and they must grow to understand the power of process.

Nurse Betty or Bob

This worker is so generous with his or her time and ready to help out a colleague that he or she doesn't get his or her own work done. Can't say no and can't budget his or her time very well. Constantly in motion, works long hours, and rarely completes his or her own to-do list. On the positive side, Nurse Bettys or Bobs can be effective as the glue for the group. There are very good sources of backdoor information in an organization, and if you allow them that outlet, meaning if you pay attention to them and seek their advice on what's going on, they're very happy. Problems may arise, however, if they become political, because they have the ability to foment distrust and disrespect among other employees. Nurse Bettys or Bobs should be allowed to provide a gathering point for the organization, but it will require close handholding to ensure that they stay on track with their tasks.

The Tattoo

This hard worker revels in bucking authority at every turn. He or she constantly frames his or her world in terms of the stupidity of those demanding something from him or her: "Here I am 90 percent done on an idea that could PUT THIS COMPANY ON THE MAP and the upstairs SUITS want me to stop everything and support last year's product." Can't be pinned down on anything. Standard response to how long something will take is "anywhere from 2 hours to 2 weeks."

This is a classic programmer mentality. The key to managing this personality type is taking them aside every few months and intellectually beating the daylights out of them. They're alpha males or females, and force is the only thing they respect. But once you've won their respect, they'll buckle down and go back to work. You have to ignore some of their bluster and constantly hold them accountable for their deliverables before you listen to their new ideas. Often their minds are racing faster than their manners or common sense. They don't need stroking; they just resist being harnessed. Unlike the Jock, the Tattoo can be channeled and more easily managed because he or she enjoys interaction.

The Shape-Up-or-Ship-Out Workers

Amadeus

This employee is the artist who deigns to walk among us. This worker has developed into a temperamental, fussy, and superstitious employee who needs constant stroking and often threatens to quit. Pronouncements are common: "The day I have to punch a timecard, I am outta here. You might as well strap an anvil to my back as make me report to some pencil-pushing accountant."

This is the classic insecure prima donna at work. Prima donnas have several issues. First, they're chronically unhappy (what is it about artists and suffering?). Second, they overvalue themselves. They see their skills as unique. Finally, they incite negativity in the organization. The three combined are a disaster. Their problems are not about the work-place; they're about the individual's need for attention, which is insatiable. If you give in and stroke them, you have to keep it up indefinitely; if you don't pay attention, they hate you for being indifferent. They continually try to rearrange the universe so that they are at the center. We've never seen people like this recover from this syndrome in the company where they develop it. Amadeuses who threaten to quit should be encouraged to do so.

Tom or Tallelulah Ticker

This worker is obsessed with his or her net worth, always has stock updates prominent on his or her computer, and is always asking about compensation issues at all-hands meetings. Constantly weighing other opportunities, this worker is like a partner who won't commit—moody, seemingly distracted, overly concerned about who gets credit for the most mundane things. His or her favorite line is, "What's in it for me?"

Life it too short to put up with people who won't commit. Ambivalence is untenable. Encourage these workers to go out and test the market or shape up. The cold water of reality will sometimes shape them up, but if it doesn't, and they decide to leave, you haven't lost too much.

Could Go Either Way

Darth Maul, the Sith Lord

You probably wouldn't deliberately hire this type of worker. He or she is quiet, brooding, even surly, and difficult to read. You may have inherited him or her from a transfer or merger. You've heard stories about his or her brains and talent, but it's unclear to you whether the Sith is more likely to save the day or go postal.

This person must be watched very carefully. Mysterious characters like this can be very disruptive and distracting in the workplace. Unfortunately, a certain percentage of these brooding, resentful people are devious, either because they resent a change that's taken place or they've got other things going on (like ripping off the company's intellectual property or trying to start their own business on your company's payroll). Farzad once worked with a guy at General Electric who actually had two jobs, and it took GE months to figure it out. He'd come in every day and put his briefcase on his desk, and then he'd sneak off to the other job.

The key to managing the Siths is to engage them and keep them busy. Do not leave them alone, because they will use the freedom as an opportunity to recruit other people to the dark side. Idle hands are the devil's playground.

The Blob

This worker's specialty has become not working. There's little doubt that this worker has the smarts and talent to do the job, but for reasons that can include distracting personal problems, depression, fear, insecurity, or sometimes good old-fashioned laziness, this worker begins to expend more energy either resisting assignments outright or gaining consensus about every decision well beyond what's required.

This is a peculiar but not uncommon problem. The phlegmatic people who don't produce either have to change and accept responsibility for their work, or they have to leave. The bright person who is resisting often is not communicating what's really wrong. It could be fear of the unknown, overwork, or something else that's tipped him or her into an atypical, unproductive state. Do a little root-cause analysis.

Nobody wants a company full of identical clones. However, it's not a good idea to ignore negative behaviors and their consequences in the workplace. They often undermine productivity, and they distract even good workers from tending to the central challenges of their jobs.

One last point about managing difficult employees. Even during the height of the "war for people" in the Silicon Valley, when skilled technology folks could virtually name their price, we encouraged our employees to go out and test the waters once a year. By "test the waters," we meant go see what kinds of jobs are out there that they might be qualified for and what kind of compensation they might pull down somewhere else. Other executives cannot believe we urged our best people to do this, but you have to live and die by transparency. Just as macroeconomists say that free and fair economies work efficiently when everyone has perfect information, so free and fair skills market-places work efficiently when everyone knows his or her own value. For every person who discovers that he or she is undervalued and deserves more compensation, there are probably three or four other people who are not concentrating on their work as they should because they're convinced they're worth so much more than they actually are. Urging them to test the waters eliminates bravado-soaked conversations that go like this: "Look, I could have a new job in 5 minutes, and if you don't agree to [give me more people/get me a corner office/whatever], that's just what I'll do." By the way, should you find yourself in the midst of this type of conversation, you can have some fun. You can reply, probably truthfully, "Oh really, I just got a call from a headhunter, too. They want a new CEO for a well-funded startup in Arizona!"

More Cultural Issues and Red Flags

If you have the conversations with your employees that we suggest in this chapter, all kinds of things are going to start falling into place. You're going to identify your immature employees—or at least the knowledge workers with immature attitudes about work. You'll have a better idea of the personality types you're dealing with and whether your odds of getting them to clean up their acts and start contributing appropriately are good, bad, or shaky. You'll probably get some sense of the signals you or the company may be giving out that give people the wrong idea.

As you sort through all this, however difficult it may be, you're steadily moving in the right direction: toward transparency. As you gain more and more information about the people working for you and how they see themselves fitting in, there are just a few more important elements to keep in mind before you really start focusing on the tactical management principles that will reorganize your workplace into a far more accountable and successful operation.

In trying to transform our clients' cultures, we have had numerous conversations with customers who mention several specific recurring issues that frequently arise in their dealings with our clients' companies. Helping you avoid these problems is why we stress some of the mechanics of our management approach later in the book. You can divide these problems into the following categories:

- Ownership issues
- Company-sponsored distractions
- Productivity feedback
- The lines between work and personal life

Ownership Issues

It's increasingly important in the knowledge workplace to reinforce something that is a legal and common-sense fact: The company owns the employees' work products, their e-mails, and the contents of their conversations with vendors, customers, and business partners conducted on the company's behalf. The company has unlimited access to the equipment it provides for the employees' use, and it has the right to review what the employees are doing with that equipment.

Employees who grouse about Big Brother "spying" on their e-mails, for example, have an unclear understanding of this simple fact. It is therefore important that it is made clear to employees from Day 1 that e-mail at work is for work. Nobody is going to care if you zap your spouse a note: "Pick up milk on the way home." However, as more and more advanced technology becomes available for intelligently corralling work products, e-mails, and other information products the company wishes to use for its strategic advantage, the more intruded upon employees may feel unless the company makes sure they are clear on this from the get-go. The company has every right to monitor Web usage, e-mails, instant messaging, and other technologies employees sometimes mistake for their own private communication spheres.

Forced Fun

It's much easier to make employees "happy" than it is to make paying customers "happy." This is a reality of life, even though it's much more important to make customers happy. During the recent period of low unemployment and skyrocketing salaries, many companies became very skewed in their thinking about this and overly concerned about showing the troops love and affection. Those days are thankfully over—for the most part. There is actually a book that was published recently called *Love Is the Killer App*, which was written by a former Yahoo executive who argues that the key to managing people is to love them.[1] We think Tina Turner said it much better: "What's love got to do with it?"

There is a need to motivate the troops during rough periods when they might get nervous and want to leave. But the more you try to replace sound strategy and good decisions with mandatory fun and morale-boosting exercises, the more you look like Nero fiddling while Rome burns. Your best people, the smart ones you really want to keep, will sense this and bail out. Your immature, less valuable employees will happily form a Conga line and dance around the Friday beer bash, telling themselves you wouldn't be spending that kind of money unless things were actually much better than they appear.

The company should not promote toys and distractions and celebrate nonevents. A basketball hoop in the parking lot, or a Ping-Pong table in the lunch room never hurt anybody. However, frequent, elaborate, organized social activities at work are a problem. Younger employees in particular will embrace fun activities that they believe ingratiate them to their managers or to other employees whose company they enjoy. In time, it becomes like playing with a 3-year-old: How do you get them to stop when you want them to stop and go back to work? And there are other new and dangerous wrinkles to workplace distractions, such as multiplayer video game sessions, "chatting" with friends or lovers, and pornography. These activities literally become addictive for some people, are obviously inappropriate in the workplace, and sap productivity.

We know a team at a major Silicon Valley company that scored its manager very low in terms of the culture he had created. After reading the survey, the manager went to his team and asked: "What can we do to make sure we have more fun around here?"

"Raise the stock price," someone yelled.

The manager was angry and retorted, "I'm serious." Well, so was the employee, it turned out, as the group discussed the situation further. What wasn't "fun" about working for this guy was that he did not demonstrate leadership or give his troops a sense of where they were going and why. They had lost confidence in him, and they felt they were being treated like children. They wanted to make money. The manager thought that all they wanted was to have fun. In the business context, we are convinced that it's success that's fun.

The Check and Balance on the Hierarchy

A healthy, dynamic, mature workplace grows and learns and is open to new options. We firmly believe that every employee should feel free to request or suggest anything that will improve productivity. This can take different forms, but all of them must be entirely visible to the employee's manager.

Any employee should be allowed to point out issues or elements that he or she believes negatively impact his or her productivity. These can be very specific, relatively minor things—for example, can we have a copy machine at my end of the floor so I don't waste half an hour a day crossing over to the other side of the building? Or they might be rather touchy, sensitive issues—for example, one employee's desire for flex-time that another employee feels will impinge on his or her productivity. We believe the workplace is for work. So we will reasonably accommodate a good, productive worker, but we will also take into account how the triathelete who wants to cut out between 12:00 and 3:00 P.M. to train, then work until 10 P.M., is affecting the whole group.

Keeping the Lines Clear

We know employees have their private lives—we have ours too—and we make a commitment to respect it. As hard-nosed as we are about the basic employer-employee covenant, we also believe the company has an interest in employing healthy, emotionally balanced people. And as vigorously as we insist that the workplace is about work, we also believe our duty is to make sure that there is a reasonable boundary between work lives and private lives.

Silicon Valley has been notorious for Friday beer bashes, and theme parties, and executive fishing trips, and tricky little perks like dentists in Winnebagos in the parking lot, and dry-cleaning pickup at the office. Part of the motive, obviously, is to keep people at the office and engaged with their coworkers to the point that they will stay in the office for extremely long periods of time.

This stuff often backfires. People get too wrapped up in artificial measures of performance and loyalty, and pretty soon they begin playing out their emotional issues in the office, which actually often interferes with their performing clear-headed work. Of course [insert despair of choice such as "I'm not married"/"I have no life"/"I'm 20 pounds overweight"], an employee may agonize, "I'm here all the time." There actually may be plenty of truth to that statement. But this lament often erupts in the context of a salary review, or a request for a transfer, or just a dramatic scene in which the employee is angling to get his or her way on something. We want to give you a raise because you are effective and productive—not because we "owe" it to you for the sheer number of hours you spend here.

We acknowledge the occasional need for crunch time, but in general we discourage marathon working sessions at the office. We want productive, efficient knowledge workers who go home at a reasonable hour every night and who relax on the weekends. We don't encourage or promote dinner meetings or off-hours socializing among employees. The more lines blur between private and work lives, the more personal and emotional issues will invade the workplace, affect morale, and interfere with general productivity. We acknowledge that some people are workaholics. Frankly, that is their business, and if it leads them to performing superhuman tasks, we're going to reward their efforts. But we aren't after that kind of culture across the board, and we aren't going to bring in a masseuse, a hairdresser, and an on-call *feng shui* advisor to make sure we support the workaholic's lifestyle.

In short: Get a life. Or keep the one you have! Philosophically, we want to make the connections between your success at work and the opportunity to improve your lifestyle as you see fit and the fruits of your labors. In other words, it's not that we don't care about work-life balance; it's that we don't want to see it played out in the workplace during the hours when we pay you to work. We don't want you taking 2 hours off for a football session every day, bringing your dog in, and holding staff meetings on Sundays while dandling your newborn on your lap. We aren't going to underwrite Friday drinking binges for you and your colleagues every week—go home and hang out with your real friends! Work efficiently during the week so you can spend Saturday at your kids' soccer games with your cell phone off. Help us make this company a success so you can take the money you make and go anywhere you want on vacation and do anything else you want.

So, your assessment and assault on creating a more accountable culture has begun. Slap on some ice blue Aqua Velva and have some honest conversations with the people who are important to you in your organization. Without a good foundation in the basic realities of the workplace, knowledge workers are apt to intellectually wander off and even wreak havoc. Get everyone to make a commitment to moving the organization forward in an accountable fashion. Then, with the next set of principles we'll discuss, you will empower your organization to reach new heights.

CHAPTER 4

The Vision Thing
The Power of Transparency

This chapter discusses two "vision things": visibility and transparency. A manager who has "visibility" can see what is going on around him or her within the organization. Visibility *is the byproduct of the clarity of information an organization is producing, the tools it's using to generate that information, and managers' sensitivities to interpreting that data. The second concept,* transparency, *is the goal. A transparent organization is a knowledge workplace nirvana where mature people at every level of the organization have insight into what's going on, they understand where the company is headed, and they can discern how they can best contribute.*

ONCE EMPLOYEES ARE CLEAR ON THINGS like why their jobs exist, what their value to the organization is, and the company's ownership of their work products, a company is ready to make a real run on transparency and begin performing at the next level. In an immature, unaccountable culture, transparency is a meaningless concept. Sulky prima donnas, process-defying mavericks, and various species of party animals who aren't being managed won't have a clue what to do in a transparent organization. The transition to an accountable workplace begins with culture, and it is turbocharged with specific tactical tools. When you bring those two elements together, you stand to create a transparent workplace in which workers have all the tools they need to do their jobs, justify their existence, and add value.

For all the excess freedom many managers give knowledge workers and teams, it is ironic that some managers, operating out of fear or insecurity, withhold key information from both their employees and upper management (or, in the case of senior executives, from everybody). They fail to broadcast corporate priorities, for example, for fear that those working on less important projects will flake out or spend all their time trying to get reassigned. They hate to be associated with bad news, so they give misleading status reports and hope some other last-minute development will divert attention from their own team's shortcomings. They reward effort instead of results because they perceive a team is working very hard and they don't want to discourage them. They become emotionally invested in struggling initiatives and suppress evidence that the efforts should be canceled.

Many of these acts are just human nature. However, each is fundamentally dishonest. And dishonesty is the enemy of a transparent organization. Particularly today, given the tremendous increase in the amount of information available about the markets and competitive spaces in which companies operate, honesty and clarity are always the best way to go. Trying to keep bad news under wraps is pointless, not to mention counterproductive. And failing to be honest about where the company is going and where its future lies leads to all kinds of bad decision making in the organization.

The best managers understand an organization's priorities, recognize opportunities, get their teams to work efficiently on problems, and react to changing situations. To do those things well, they need what business pundits increasingly call "visibility." Like ship captains, to be successful, managers need to know where they are going and the options and alternative routes for getting there. Managers need their crew to follow their orders, and they need to be ready to adjust if a storm whips up or a tailwind settles in. If the ship is sitting in the middle of a fog bank with no instruments, the odds of doing any or all of the above decline precipitously.

We don't know when everyone started using the term *visibility* in the business context. Not so long ago we just used to call this "knowing what's going on," as in, "We need to get rid of that guy. He doesn't know what the hell is going on." In any event, we will go with convention and use this term to describe a manager's ability to see and understand some pretty basic things about the organization, such as whether the manager's people are working on the things they should be working on and whether they're doing so efficiently.

When an organization's culture is off kilter, the reason is often that managers are looking at the wrong things. They may be looking for bodies in chairs at all hours instead of tangible evidence of progress. They may be looking for signs of happiness in talented but difficult employees who they are terrified may leave, rather than motivating valuable employees by clearly laying out challenges and opportunities. They may be content with vague status reports, rather than pressing team members to speak up about possible roadblocks as they occur. On the other side of the table, immature, toxic-tending employees are prone to manipulating information to suit their own needs and desires.

It's fair to point out that even those managers who develop and encourage a professional, accountable workplace and who understand the concept of adult supervision still struggle with visibility in the knowledge workplace because the output of their workers is difficult to measure on a daily basis. Widgets aren't dropping off the end of the assembly line and into a bucket for counting. Sales aren't going ka-ching in the cash register as the tally soars. A 6-month initiative may not look all that more "done" to the naked eye in month 4 than it did in month 1, even if progress is right on track.

In the next few chapters, we are going to lay out some very specific tactical steps that will dramatically improve your visibility and create a more transparent workplace. As you'll soon see, the unifying tool in transparency-enhancing tactics is the weekly status report. The status report is a manager's eyeball into the organization—its priorities, its processes, and its progress. The next few chapters will demonstrate how to use these weekly reports to keep an organization accountable without stifling or micromanaging the creativity and enthusiasm of a knowledge workforce. To assess where you stand right now, however, we thought we'd share what our customers tell us are four basic warning signs that a company doesn't have the visibility it should:

- Managers discover people working on the wrong things.
- Teams keep reinventing the wheel.
- Initiatives are pursued without a definition of how progress will be identified.
- Workers confuse inputs and outcomes.

"And Just What Exactly Are You Doing?" Working on the Wrong Things

As a manager of a knowledge organization, your company has given you control over some valuable resources: time, people, and money. You need to make sure that you spend those resources on the things that will give the highest return. That's your basic deal.

When we talk to knowledge workplace managers about the problems that bedevil them, one of the most interesting complaints is the frequent discovery that people are working on the "wrong things." It sounds sort of ridiculous. Yet, we hear all the time about rogue initiatives that germinate inside large R&D organizations, for example. Managers get caught up in the enthusiasm of aggressive go-getters and start diverting resources from approved initiatives into far-out concepts for markets the company doesn't even address—or want to address.

Other variations on "wrong things" include: tinkering with and perfecting very minor elements of a task that is supposed to be completed instead of clearing the deck for a more important initiative; methodically focusing on minor but "doable" customer issues, while procrastinating in attacking more complex and important problems for more significant customers; and—a very common one—ignoring components of the job a worker or team dislikes while overdoing another component. At Niku, we had a classic example of this. We had a business development executive who had an explicit two-part mission: to acquire companies and develop partner deals, and to manage the integration of those acquisitions and the progress of the deals. He loved making deals. He hated managing the details. We could not digest all that he was bringing us, in part because he was ignoring the fallout of the deals. The upshot was that at least half the time (although his tenure with us was brief), he was working on "the wrong things."

To fix this, you need to make sure that you are doing what matters, as we discuss in detail in the next chapter.

What Goes Around Comes Around: Reinventing the Wheel

In scientific and engineering fields, large databases of established literature aid knowledge workers in finding out if the research they're working on has been tackled before, and if so, how. It's literally become as easy as a few taps on the keyboard to generate every article published in the scientific press about a certain biotechnology approach to curing a specific disease, for example, complete with precisely described papers on the techniques used, and even commentary on alternate theories or techniques used in competing laboratories. Wouldn't it be great if every field had such a resource? Imagine going to a database and typing in: "marketing strategies for rolling out artificial popcorn flavoring" and getting a few hundred options to study, both within your company and from others. Instead, so much knowledge work seems to start from pure scratch.

The second widespread frustration we perceive in knowledge workplaces is the "reinventing-the-wheel" problem. It's one thing to be blindsided by a competitor who you didn't realize was working on the same type of product or service as you, but it's devastating to learn that your own people were unwittingly competing against each other with similar efforts that split your organization's resources. Or to learn only well after the fact that you employed people with experience who could have added value to an activity, but those employees never knew the activity existed. Or, even more commonly, to find out that your organization keeps investing time in "inventing" new processes that have already been developed and could easily be used for new initiatives.

In each of these cases, your organization lacks transparency. Don't fall into the common trap of thinking that because you're a knowledge organization, everything your knowledge organization faces is different and thus requires an entirely unique solution. In fact, the processes your organization uses—or should use—to solve problems are usually the same.

For example, let's say you own a party-planning company. Creativity and one-of-a-kind events are your business. However, when planning and giving a party, you always need to meet with the client, plan the party, schedule it, review your plans with the client, prepare the menu, order the food and decorations, prepare the meal, then do the setup, serving, and cleanup. Skip one step, and the party will not turn out so well. Do all your people know that this is the right sequence of steps for planning and giving a party? Do they take advantage of this knowledge and experience and follow these same steps on new engagements? Or do they start from scratch at every new opportunity? In organizations that reject process management, steps that seem obvious to take to experienced people inside the organizations are not taken by other people in the company, causing needless gaffes all the time. Processes are the key to repeatable success. We'll show how process should be implemented in a knowledge organization in Chapter 6.

Half Empty or Half Full? How Should Progress Be Tracked?

Ask some managers about the status of programs inside their knowledge-based organizations, and our customers tell us they often get dialogue that sounds like it's from a television show featuring a small-town sheriff walking down Main Street.

> **"How's business, Floyd?"**
> **"Mighty fine, Andy. Can't complain!"**
> **"Well, good morning, Aunt Bea. How is that quilt for the county fair coming along?"**
> **"I think we'll make it, Andy. We're sure workin' hard!"**

With no disrespect intended to the fine citizens of Mayberry, R.F.D., these answers don't cut it. The lack of easy metrics for pegging progress to programs powered by knowledge work is no excuse for just wishin' and hopin' and prayin' they get done.

These genial responses pass for status reports. Actually, they are more like enthusiasm reports, and you will never have transparency if you are content to accept enthusiasm reports instead of true status reports. We are going to show you how to fix that problem in Chapter 7.

Another status report problem is the dumptruck report. Bernhard Vieregge, director of group strategy at T-Mobile, the wireless division of Deutsche Telekom, tells a cautionary story about status reports. Vieregge is responsible for identifying and developing synergies among T-Mobile's different business units to decrease their operating expenses. "If you go to your boss's weekly staff meeting and a colleague presents three pages of status information," says Vieregge, "then there is great pressure for you to produce four pages the next week. Pretty soon the status report stack is approaching 100 pages per week." Nobody can read all that, and most of the data in the reports are simply snapshots of the work in progress, and they don't convey actual progress, or, more importantly, time to completion. The manager ends up sitting there with that 100-page stack he or she can't possibly read and asking for a summary. Loosely translated, this is the summary: "I think we'll make it, Andy. We're sure working hard."

Confusing Inputs and Outcomes

Knowledge work transforms an organization's knowledge into business value. Knowledge is the input; business value is the outcome. Customers pay for the value, not the input. It takes wisdom to mix the right combination of inputs to yield the correct, profitable outcome. Our customers complain that these two functions often proceed independently in their organizations, leading to disaster. The worst case is a dissatisfied customer on whom they lose money.

Let's go back to the party planner. Your inputs are your time, the Rolodex you stole off Martha's desk, your rented tents, crystal, flatware, linens, your experience, skills, planning capabilities, dazzling interpersonal skills, know-how, your cooks, cater-waiters, and other staff. Your outcome is a successful party, as is shown in Figure 4–1.

You transform these inputs into business value: a party that will be talked about for a long, long time. How you achieve this transformation defines how good a party planner you are. If you serve the same teeny weeny dogs with purple ketchup that were such a hit for little Dougie's fifth birthday party to the Gorzynski's fiftieth anniversary dinner, you won't get asked back. That is obvious. If you focus on only the inputs—in this case trying to reuse a party template that worked for a previous party—you will fail.

If you choose to focus on only the outcome, you will blaze a different path to failure. You may be able to magically transform your clients' vision into a dream reception for their only daughter's wedding, complete with pink and white bunting tacked to anything that doesn't move, a wedding cake topped with custom-made Lladro figurines of the bride and groom, and the first song played by the band being the one the

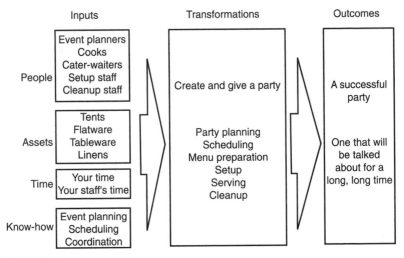

Figure 4–1

father of the bride wrote the day his daughter was born (my goodness, we're getting a little *verklempt*), but achieving this vision may not make you any money, and it might take up so much of your time that you lose several other clients.

The party details *are* very different from client to client—but a single process that includes discussion and calibration of your capabilities with the customer's desires would enable you to deliver two great parties. And because you were methodically following a successful process, you would have calculated the input costs and the value provided and made sure you made a profit.

We should point out that the problems in the above scenario were exactly the problems the now-defunct dot.coms failed to solve. The dot.coms were so outcome oriented and underwritten by so much dumb money that they paid no attention to profits, only to acquiring happy happy customers. As a friend of ours once said about the home delivery service Kosmo: "Aren't they the people who charged $19.95 to deliver $20 bills to your house?"

Knowledge-based organizations need to understand how inputs will combine to achieve a desired outcome. If the desired outcome is a great wedding cake, does that mean you need a pastry chef as well as a cook? If you run a software company, when should investing resources in solving one customer's unique demands take precedence over finishing a feature that would make the program more valuable for 80 percent of your customers? Does delaying the signing of a contract over language that represents, at most, a small risk, justify delaying the first investment dollars? The answer to all these questions is: It depends. That's why you need managers with good visibility into their organizations.

Unfortunately, our customers say they are constantly running into situations in which the input folks aren't talking to the outcome folks until bad decisions have been made. This happens because neither side really understands the big picture. Managers have made faulty assumptions, which were compounded by not staying on top of both input and outcome elements. We'll discuss the different ways a knowledge work organization can work smarter in Chapter 8.

The Accountability Management Solution: Part II

In Chapter 3, we talked about the cultural foundation a company needs to set in order to embrace accountability. These are the first, second, and third principles of the Accountability Management System.

To attack the lack of transparency in organizations that are suffering these problems, you need to pay attention to four additional principles: alignment, efficiency, measurability, and effectiveness. These problems and their solutions are shown in Table 4–1. These are the subjects of principles 4 through 7 in our Accountability Management System.

An organization that is transparent understands its progress and can spot problems in real time, as they occur. This allows the organization

Table 4-I: Visibility Problems and Solutions

Problem	Solution	Accountability Management System Principle	Benefit
Working on the wrong things	Portfolio management	Do what matters	Alignment
Always reinventing the wheel	Process management	Do it right	Efficiency
No clear measure of progress	Progress tracking	Track progress	Measurability
Confusing inputs and outcomes	Knowledge management	Work smart	Effectiveness

to react to new situations and to new opportunities and rejigger things to keep everything on track. A transparent organization is able to show the executives the real-time status of their high-priority initiatives.

The way you achieve transparency is to actively *manage* your knowledge workers and programs. The discussion that follows, in which the next four principles of our Accountability Management System are described, will tell you just how to do that. These steps consist of the tasks you must undertake and the management processes you must adopt in order to actually achieve a productive workplace and have motivated employees. (The next four chapters will talk about how to gain visibility into the knowledge workplace.)

The first step is to align your programs and initiatives with your corporate goals. To do this, you need first to recognize and accept that no company can do everything. Therefore, management needs to set and broadcast corporate priorities, and not interrupt mission-critical activities with low-priority work. Individual contributors are rewarded for completing important targets first, before advancing new ideas or pursuing low-priority endeavors. Our shorthand for this is "Do what matters." This alignment is implemented through *portfolio management*, which is the process of creating a framework for priorities and actively managing workload within that framework. Articulating the company's priorities provides a roadmap for accountability to the organization, and aligning all existing work within those priorities highlights redundant and unnecessary activities.

The second step is to set up a plan and follow it—in other words, make sure you're doing it right. Process is as valuable in the knowledge-based workplace as routine is in the medical arts workplace. In both areas standardized procedures yield consistent and accurate results. Every important activity performed in a functioning, efficient knowledge workplace requires sequential steps and coordinated effort. Management must expect rigorous, structured project management discipline; however, it should encourage employees to own and constantly improve the processes of their actual work. Process management attacks the "reinventing-the-wheel" problem by establishing best practices, and it provides a good visibility mechanism by demanding periodic reporting of data.

Process is often an unpopular concept, and that is unfortunate because it has real power. Process management eliminates the "launch-and-forget" problems that plague so much of knowledge work. The importance of this step cannot be overstated. Without a standardized process for doing and reporting on work, your organization does not have a common vocabulary with which it can define and measure itself.

Third, to improve visibility, track progress. The company must utilize not just time but progress tracking to improve the total company visibility and flexibility in the context of a dynamic and challenging business environment. The company can't assess and improve upon what it can't measure. Thus managers must not only demand an accounting of time spent but an estimate of time to completion. Instead of optimistically sending your knowledge workers off on their merry way with a basket of goodies for Granny, progress tracking allows you to put a GPS device in the picnic basket so that you can see where the employees are and how far they have to go at all times. If the tracking device stalls or loses its signal, you can launch a search party to locate employees and get the project back on track.

Finally, once the first three steps have been accomplished, the organization can leap forward with its employees working smarter, sharing knowledge, and seeking knowledge. Some types of knowledge can be encoded in processes. Other types of knowledge have to be experienced. Knowledge organizations need to foster ways of collaborating to share that type of knowledge. That will help everyone in your organization work smarter, from the most callow greenhorn to the most grizzled expert.

Things Go Better at Coke

Let's discuss a transparent organization. Richard Whelchel is a manager at the Coca-Cola Bottling Company Consolidated. It is the second-largest Coca-Cola systems bottler, with approximately $1.5 billion in revenues. It employs 6000 people and serves primarily the southeastern United States. Whelchel is responsible for overseeing projects that range in size from a few hundred thousand dollars to a few million dollars. When he joined the organization, he could repeat, almost word for word, the stories that Chuck had told me: white-knuckle worry about critical initiatives, lots of overworked people, little quantitative data about deployments and progress. He was unsure what his people were working on. He was unsure of the status of their work. He didn't know if things would finish on time. It was an opaque organization.

Whelchel set about gaining visibility by implementing the Accountability Management System, Part 2. Of course, he didn't call it the "Accountability Management System." He's an intuitive practitioner of adult supervision—so he calls it "common sense." Whelchel is also the kind of manager who takes care to give the credit to his manager for supporting him, as well as to his team, which is dedicated to improving the organization.

For his first step, he identified his organization's priorities and organized them in a portfolio, where everyone could see them. "To get the biggest bang for your buck, make sure you're working on the right projects, the ones that are strategically aligned with your corporate strategy. There has to be a way to understand which projects have the best return on investment and those that will affect the bottom line most quickly," Whelchel says.

Second, he institutionalized best practices in the form of business processes and project management processes. Whelchel says, "You must have a life cycle or a methodology for whatever you do to benefit your business. Then you need to make these standard methodologies repeatable. So you can deliver success not just by project but across the whole enterprise. . . . If you have a process, your people can use it. If it's good, you can improve it. If it's not, you can change it. It's your way out of the bog."

Third, for every activity that was in his portfolio, he asked his people to track their progress. He asked them to report on a weekly basis what they were working on and how much further they had to go. This gave him a basic measurement, a yardstick, with which to track the progress of the company as a whole. He verified alignment, and he determined who was working on what, and where each person was on the road to completion of key tasks. According to Whelchel, progress tracking is "a way to understand where you are and make reasonable adjustments as needed in the early stages of a project's development." He could also spot bottlenecks and identify points at which things were starting to go off track. This early-warning system enabled him to react to problems immediately. He was gaining more detailed visibility.

The payoff has been significant. When he arrived in the organization in 1999, he had no understanding of the company's project success rate. He says, "We started off with absolutely no knowledge of where we were. That was the bog, so to speak. We really had no measure of how we did."

In the year 2000, he could report a 38 percent project success rate. Of the 45 key projects the company wanted completed by that year, 17 were completed on time—a modest success and a significant improvement over the previous year.

In the year 2001, he was able to significantly improve his project success rate, to 61 percent. Of the 46 key projects targeted, 28 were completed. Also, his organization was able to absorb 11,000 hours of unplanned project activity by reacting to emergencies, incorporating new opportunities, and implementing new strategic initiatives. "That to me was an astounding ratio, an astounding number. We knew we were in a 60 to 70 percent delivery position throughout the year," he adds.

This is real visibility. In this organization, the grown-ups are in charge.

Do What Matters
The Power of Setting and Broadcasting Priorities

Some KNOWLEDGE WORKERS understandably feel as though they work not in a cubicle but on the narrow lip of a frying pan with a roaring fire below. We were once advising a human resources organization in a scanner company about standardized business processes. One day, the CEO realized that his company did not have a standardized employee appraisal process, and he panicked and barked an order to the manager to get one, stat. So the entire organization, all three of them, dropped everything to work on one. The CEO's panic quickly subsided, but for a 3-week period the team did not do anything else, including process any new hires, until it delivered that employee appraisal process. Therefore, the new hires did not get paid. Then, the CEO yelled at them for that.

This is called "*I Dream of Jeannie* Initiative Management." Want to add a new initiative to an organization's task list? Fold your arms, smile, and blink. The approach assumes magic powers and infinite resources. Therefore, it's up to your reports to figure out from where the resources will come to make it happen, or what will not get done, or what will be late, or any other troublesome details.

No company can do everything. Yet so many of our customers find themselves with a kudzu garden of distracting, low-value, or offtrack projects, initiatives, and activities that have bloomed in their knowledge workplaces. Most were fertilized by plenty of enthusiasm but insufficient analysis. When knowledge workers ask their managers for help in ranking the projects, they're told they're all critical. Something's got to give, but too often it boils down to the program least likely to attract a senior executive's wrath.

The antidote to this situation is portfolio management. In the knowledge arena, the portfolio consists of the initiatives, opportunities, programs, and other activities that the organization is working on. Knowledge-based initiatives may include a PR campaign to raise awareness of a company to a certain customer population, for example. Or it might be a program to reduce cycle time in contract reviews. Or it may be a new financial planning service.

All of these things are expected to drive business value by either increasing revenue or reducing costs, and they all require resources. Portfolio management means constantly reevaluating the mix of initiatives and programs underway and making sure the company is on track to get a worthwhile return from those efforts. Existing activities may be rescoped, replanned, killed, accelerated, broadened, or told to keep chugging along. It also means analyzing which new opportunities are the right ones to go after with the resources that are available. By actually valuing initiatives and programs individually, managers can make good decisions at an appropriate level.

Setting and Communicating Priorities

Portfolio management is a list of projects on steroids. It is the art of deploying your employees' talents to deliver the most value. It's the tie between what to do and how to do it, as shown in Figure 5–1.

The best-run organizations specifically create and articulate a portfolio. A portfolio consists of all your initiatives, programs, subprograms,

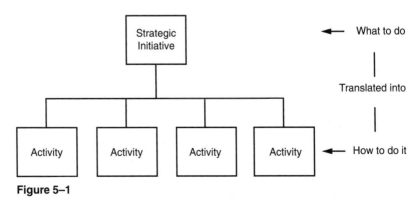

Figure 5–1

opportunities, activities, tasks, projects, cases, and campaigns. By putting all of your work into a portfolio, and explicitly tying the goals to the implementation activities for the goals, you can manage your work at a business level. You can balance costs and benefits, and talk about adding business value instead of task completion dates.

The most successful organizations then broadcast this portfolio up and down the ladder. By doing so, they discourage random acts of work-summoning by roving bands of senior executives with pet projects. They also discourage secret rogue projects. They focus the entire company on doing the work that matters, and their openness about what matters allows the organization to manage itself and stay on track.

The process of developing a good portfolio involves describing the organization's work as it is, then as it should be based on its goals, and then merging the two.

Step I. Define the Portfolio

Our first introduction to how helpful portfolio management could be was during a consulting engagement in the 1980s, with a manufacturing company in southern California. Let's call this company Allis Manufacturing. The company had an old medical device manufacturing floor, and a new CFO. The old CFO was gone, and with him the company believed had gone several million dollars artfully removed from the company over a number of years. The company wanted the new CFO to tighten all of the financial business processes. They needed help to improve and implement these processes, as well as install a new computer system to automate their implementation.

The first step that the CFO took was to simply define the portfolio— all of the activities that his organization was responsible for. A portion of his portfolio is shown in Table 5–1.

A knowledge manager can use a portfolio in this very simple state as a snapshot of the organization. A good portfolio, in the defining phase, has the following characteristics:

- It identifies every single activity. All sanctioned activities should show up on the portfolio. No secret skunk works are allowed.
- It identifies responsibilities. Every activity has an owner, who is the person responsible for the delivery of the value.

Table 5-I: Allis Manufacturing Portfolio, Step I

Program	Sponsor or Customer	Time Frame	Manager
Review cash management processes. Suggest improvements.	Board of directors	1 month	Hans
Implement financial accounting system.	Board of directors	3 months	CFO
Perform month-end close.	CEO	Must be completed 3 days after month end	Abby
...			
...			
...			

- It identifies customers. Every activity has a customer—that is, the person or group for whom this activity is performed.
- It is explicitly communicated. After assembly, the portfolio should be communicated, posted, and reviewed in meetings.

Step 2. Review the Portfolio

By putting everything in one portfolio, a manager can more easily spot redundant or unnecessary work activities. One of our customers in the insurance industry discovered, a few days after developing a portfolio, that five different organizations were engaged in the same type of exploratory work. All five organizations were separately pursuing a search for a collaboration tool to allow their people to work together more efficiently.

And people wonder where Scott Adams gets his material for the *Dilbert* cartoon.

Managers should review their portfolio once a week, and they should include an update in their own status reports to their managers. This is an ongoing activity. The key to doing this is to link the portfolio with everyone's status reports. The program managers (the people responsible for implementing particular programs) should report status on a weekly basis regarding the programs for which they are responsible. They will update the knowledge manager with the following information:

- Progress: What progress was made on the program last week
- Plans: What progress is expected to be made on the program this week
- Problems: Any issues that must be brought to the knowledge manager's attention

The manager will then update the portfolio, particularly the time frame, using this information. The format of the status report is shown in Table 5–2, which uses examples from the Allis Manufacturing Portfolio.

The first and second steps in portfolio management—define and review—give knowledge managers a framework in which to manage knowledge work, clearly assign responsibility, provide a feedback loop, ensure that everyone is working on the right things, and potentially reduce an organization's workload.

This portfolio allowed the new Allis CFO to create an accountable, functioning organization in a very challenging environment. Within a few months, the company was able to improve its credit rating, its major suppliers had taken them off of credit hold, and the accounts payable (A/P) and accounts receivable (A/R) organizations were fully staffed and working efficiently.

Checklist for Reviewing a Portfolio
- Is every activity in the portfolio represented on your status report?
- Does the status of each activity on the status report show progress, plans, and problems?
- Does each activity owner report his or her activities on his or her weekly status report to you?
- Do you review your status report with your boss once a week?
- Do you review your people's status reports once a week?
- After receiving your people's status reports, do you update your portfolio with any changed dates?

Step 3. Measure the Value of and Prioritize the Portfolio

The next step is to prioritize the work in the portfolio. This action helps an organization allocate the most time to the most important activities. According to John Elliott, managing director at Bear Stearns,

Table 5–2: A Sample Status Report

Program Name	Progress: What Progress Was Made on This Program Last Week? What Key Milestones Were Attained? What Key Deliverables or Sign-Offs Were Obtained?	Plans: What Is Expected to Happen This Week? Which Important Activities Are Expected to Be Accomplished?	Problems: What Problems Exist That Need the Manager's Help to Resolve? What Show Stoppers?
Review cash management processes. Suggest improvements.	Reviewed payment, receivables, and cash application processes.	Review treasury processes.	No owner for treasury processes—who to designate?
Implement financial accounting system.	Defined schedule and responsibilities. Scheduled training for next week.	Install software for training class. Train all users.	Not enough disk space in the computer. Need to buy more or accomplish training offline.
Perform month-end close	All pro forma statements generated and reviewed.	Close books, and reconcile accounts.	None.

...

"A portfolio prevents managers from looking at individual projects in a vacuum. Instead of optimizing each separate project, managers can start optimizing the entire portfolio. It fosters communication in the organization, as well as with the business units."

Managers must be willing to rank the relative importance of the initiatives, programs, and other efforts under their control. This has two difficult elements. First, many managers loathe identifying any one task or project as less important than another in their domain because they fear they'll paint a target on the backs of people or programs. The reasoning goes like this: "I'll be damned if I'm going to lose people from my lean, mean organization while Sullivan over there in finance, who's been padding his organization for years, offers up a couple deadbeats and that's it." They prefer the notion that everything on the list is as important as everything else, or it wouldn't be on the list.

Do not be swayed by these arguments. This is not negotiable and everyone must do it. This is what being a manager is about, making choices, often difficult choices, when resources are not infinite.

The other thing that's difficult about this is that ranking priorities is a step you don't want to broadcast. This step is crucial for opportunity management and resource allocation. However, there is nothing to be gained, and much to be lost, by publishing the portfolio, with each initiative ranked, to the rank and file. Workers on low-ranked projects and programs will become nervous, paranoid, and distracted—often for no good reason, as there may, in fact, be sufficient resources for the company to pursue most if not all of its current lineup. Nevertheless, the portfolio is solely a management tool. Much of the same data will, in fact, be available to everyone, but it will arrive in a different format—the resource allocation chart we'll describe in a minute.

In order to prioritize a portfolio, you must be able to measure the value of each program. You can define a value by simply adding up the benefits and subtracting the costs. The most important programs are those that deliver the highest value to the organization.

You need to calculate a benefit and cost for each program. Real values are absolutely necessary, as we will see. Costs are usually easier to estimate than benefits. You can estimate a cost based on the number of people assigned, multiplied by the number of days they will work on the program, multiplied by each person's daily wage, with an overhead rate added, if you have that information. Any other costs such as the costs of equipment, materials, travel, contractor charges are added to come up with a total program cost.

Every program in the portfolio should have a quantifiable benefit. If a benefit cannot be quantified or even articulated, it begs the question: Why are we doing this? If you, as a knowledge manager, cannot assign a quantifiable benefit to an activity that is costing the organization something, what does that say about the program? We think it says, "There is no clear goal." If a program's stakeholder suggests that the benefit of his or her pet program is nothing more than "better information," "increased efficiency," or "timelier status," and he or she cannot quantify the benefits further, then he or she should be asked to try again. Without numbers, managers will be reduced to making silly statements like, "This is going to be big! Big! BIG!" If you, as a knowledge manager, can't define a benefit for a program, you should go to the customer and clearly ask, "What benefit do you expect to receive if I do this thing?" If you do not have access to the customer, you should go to sales or to some other customer-facing organization and jointly work out the benefit.

Break down benefits into two buckets: increased revenues and decreased costs. For increased revenues, there are both hard and soft benefits. For customer-paid programs, the benefit is simply the price the client has agreed to pay. This is a direct increase in revenues. For marketing programs or other programs with a potential for generating revenue, the benefits are softer. Examples of both hard and soft benefits in terms of increased revenues are shown in Table 5–3.

For decreased costs, there are both hard and soft savings. Examples of hard savings include reduced headcount and reduced capital expenses. Soft savings come from increased efficiencies, decreased error rates, and so on. See Table 5–4 for some examples of cost savings.

Table 5–3: Hard and Soft Benefits of Increased Revenues

Hard Benefits	Soft Benefits
Increased sales	Increased number of potential customers
Increased margins	Increased likelihood to buy
Increased size of sales	Increased customer satisfaction
Reduced customer returns	Increased number of repeat customers

Table 5–4: Hard and Soft Savings from Decreased Costs

Hard Savings	Soft Savings
Reduced headcount	Increased efficiency
Reduced capital expenses	Decreased number of errors
Reduced overhead	Decreased legal fees
Reduced facilities charges	Increased transaction processing speed
Reduced IT charges	
Reduced contractor charges	

Soft savings can be realized in such ways as making a knowledge worker more efficient. If you free up 1 hour of a person's time, you could potentially save however much it costs you to employ that person for 1 hour. However, the assumption is that that person's 1 hour of new free time will be well utilized. A poorly managed person might simply end up enjoying an extra hour of online gambling instead of recapturing productive time. That is why all soft savings should be discounted. A hard savings of $100 equals $100. A soft savings of $100 should be discounted, by some percentage, roughly corresponding to the probability that the efficiency gains will translate into savings. We've seen discounts of 50 to 75 percent in this area.

In valuing the programs in the portfolio, the key is to force some value analysis on every item. Knowledge workers rebel at this. "Everyone knows" you have to have sales brochures for a catering company, for example, but how can we tell if one of those brochures might generate 5 huge parties or 43 small ones? How can you quantify that kind of marketing value in a portfolio?

Well, you can start on the cost side. For an existing brochure, how many are you producing, and at what cost? What is the approximate number of people exposed to the brochure per quarter, based on your existing distribution system? Do you have any historical response rate numbers? If so, how many of the respondees became sales, and how large were the average sales?

Answers to those questions should yield the data for some basic calculations about what that brochure is worth to the business. Granted, some of this is based on soft numbers, so the values should be represented as ranges. The statement "Designing new brochures will get us $7,675.48

worth of new business within 3 weeks" sounds absurdly specific. In contrast, the statement "A new brochure could bring in between $5000 and $10,000 of new business within 3 weeks" sounds more plausible. Both statements are consistent; the latter acknowledges the uncertainty of the data.

Once each program's costs and benefits are defined, they should be added to the portfolio. They should be kept up to date, using the information from the status reports that the knowledge manager gets from he or her direct reports. The portfolio is then prioritized by ordering all programs, from most valuable to least valuable. In an ideal world, a program's priority correlates to the value it provides to the organization. The more value a program brings, the higher its priority.

With a prioritized portfolio, knowledge managers have a mechanism for aligning the organization with the most important work. They can see, clearly and in one place, all of the activities in their organization and the value each activity brings. By rank ordering them in priority order, they have a tool to make sure they spend time on the most valuable activities.

But the best thing about a prioritized portfolio is that it allows a knowledge manager to engage his or her own manager in an intelligent conversation about program priorities, due dates, and tradeoffs. If a knowledge manager has a portfolio, and the boss does a drive-by and says, "Do it now!" the knowledge manager can start framing the discussion by saying, "OK, is this more or less important than this other program?" The knowledge manager can work with his or her boss to verify that the organization is aligned with the boss's wishes and that he or she is spending resources on the highest-priority activities.

Checklist for Prioritizing a Portfolio

- Do all programs have a cost?
- Are soft savings discounted?
- Do all programs have a benefit?
- Are soft benefits discounted?
- Do all programs have a value?
- Are all programs sorted, in order, from highest value to lowest value?
- Is the greatest percentage of resources allocated to the highest-value activities?
- Are low- or negative-value activities being rethought?

Step 4. Categorize the Work

Through step 3, the portfolio has been developed from the bottom up. Step 4 is designed as a reality check. In this step, categorization, you compare your portfolio with another portfolio, one that you develop from the top down. To create the top-down portfolio, you start with your company's strategic goals and identify all activities your organization should be doing to support those goals. Then you compare that top-down portfolio with your current portfolio to see if your organization is in alignment.

Start with your management objectives, your job description, or anything else that describes what you and your organization should be doing. A CEO might take a more global approach to dividing up the company into functions he or she considers core, for example, using the *balanced scorecard approach*, a strategic management system introduced by Kaplan and Norton.[1] Many of our customers use this. It categorizes goals into four buckets: customer, financial, learning and growth, and internal business processes. *Customer goals* describe targets like customer satisfaction, retention, and market share. *Financial goals* relate to profitability, cash flow, and other financial measures. *Learning and growth goals* deal with training and implementing better systems. *Internal business process goals* deal with the internal activities and financial goals. Specific goals are defined for each of the buckets, plans are implemented to achieve the goals, and a feedback loop is implemented to verify goal attainment. If your company uses a balanced scorecard, your organization should be busy supporting one or more of these goals.

In any event, to create a top-down portfolio, start with a strategic goal or one of your management objectives. Add all of the activities that your organization should be doing in order to support these goals or objectives. Link these activities to the goal. Do this for all goals. A very specific item under "learning and growth," for example, may be improving diversity and implementing diversity training. Under the activities that support that goal might be an all-hands lunchtime seminar, half-hour breakout sessions for every department, and a poster series promoting the value of diversity within the organization.

You should now have a portfolio that lists all the activities your organization should be engaged in. Compare this top-down portfolio to the portfolio that you have developed through the defining, reviewing, and prioritizing phases. Some of your existing activities may actually appear so far outside the realm of your top-down portfolio that you should seriously consider dropping them. You also are probably missing some activities. Add these activities to your portfolio. You are explicitly aligning your organization's activities to your company's strategic goals. You now have a way of showing your boss how many of your people are working on the things that the company cares the most about.

To see this point more clearly, take a look at Figure 5–2, which shows a portfolio before categorization. There are 19 activities in this portfolio. After categorization, the portfolio looks like Figure 5–3, and intelligent statements can be made such as the following:

- Almost half of my organization's activities support the development of new products (9/19 = 47 percent).
- Of my organization's total activities, 15 percent are devoted to expense reduction.
- Of my organization's total efforts, 100 percent are aligned with achieving our strategic goals.

Without categorization, managers drown in details and cannot see the patterns. With it, however, you have a framework for providing the right level of detail to the right people. Further, you can share resource allocations and make sound decisions to shift resources up and down the hierarchy. That's because a worker is not as threatened by knowing

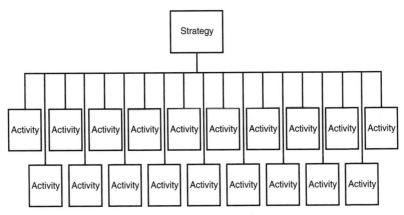

Figure 5–2

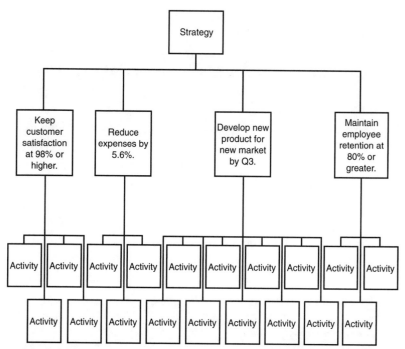

Figure 5–3

that he or she is involved in an activity that represents only 10 percent of the company's resource allocations (an individual may have a very inexpensive and cost-effective, absolutely vital function) as he or she would be to hear that his or her project was ranked in the bottom 10 percent of the company's priorities. Armed with this kind of data, managers can work with their people to develop new efficiency goals, point out rogue efforts, or discuss why people are being moved from one project to another.

Checklist for Categorizing a Portfolio

- Does your portfolio include all of your management objectives?
- Does your portfolio include all strategic initiatives that are part of your responsibility?
- Are all activities and programs in your portfolio linked to either a management objective or a strategic initiative?
- Do all objectives and strategic initiatives include at least one activity?

- Are you devoting the most resources to the most important objectives and strategic initiatives?
- Do you have enough resources to achieve your objectives?

Step 5. Balance the Portfolio

If you have made it this far, you have achieved 80 percent of the value that portfolio management can bring you. You have a list of all of the activities in your organization. You have a process to review the portfolio, highlighting unneeded and redundant projects, and keeping your portfolio up to date. You've prioritized the entries in your portfolio by ranking them in terms of value. This has forced alignment with your customers as well as giving you an opportunity to analyze tradeoffs. Finally, categorization has provided you with a means to gain strategic focus and to become more proactive about what your organization should be doing. It provides you with a response to whatever your bosses are telling you to do, or your customers are screaming at you to do, or your knowledge workers want to work on.

The next step is to balance your portfolio. This step is a refinement of your categorization step. According to a portfolio manager in a strategy group at a large U.K. bank, this step is usually completed iteratively with the previous step. Categorization and balancing go hand in hand. "We found we needed to go through this iteration since balancing refines the categorization," said the portfolio manager. This manager had been working on the development and implementation of this portfolio for 9 months when we spoke to him. Steps 1 and 2 were simple. He said, "It took us only a few weeks to get the portfolio defined and to institutionalize a process with which each manager could update it. Prioritization was more difficult, since it required the definition of a consistent means of valuing opportunities and initiatives. We needed 6 months to develop such a methodology and roll it out." Categorization and balancing came next, and since categorization begged the question about their strategic focus, categorization and balancing were constantly informing the bank's stalled balanced-scorecard implementation. The portfolio manager credited the portfolio definition project with providing the bank with more strategic focus overall.

Balance requires feedback. It requires feedback from above, from the strategic direction. It requires that the manager feed back the information to executives about the relative resource allocations across the different strategic initiatives. For example, the manager should ask, "Does it make sense that almost half of my organization's activities support the development of new products? Should it be 75 percent? 25 percent?" This is a question that must be answered in dialog with management and executives.

Balance also requires feedback from below, from the organization itself. Do you have a balanced portfolio in terms of the right mix of activities? Do your activities deliver their results in a steady stream, rather than in a big clump, all at once? Do your activities use resources in a balanced way, or are your people playing lots of solitaire for half the month, then pulling all-nighters the rest of the time?

Checklist for Balancing a Portfolio

- Have you reviewed your portfolio with your boss?
- Has your boss agreed with your resource allocations across categories?
- Are you balancing the use of your resources, with steady utilization rates across time periods?
- Are you delivering value in a balanced way, with steady delivery across time periods?
- Do you have enough resources to achieve your objectives in the right time frame?

Step 6. Manage Your Portfolio

The last step is to manage the portfolio. In this step, the portfolio management process is integrated with the budgeting process as well as with opportunity analysis. This is the last step in portfolio management, and it helps knowledge managers run their organization in lock step with their company's strategic planning process. It also helps knowledge managers evaluate new opportunities and efficiently decide if and where they fit.

During the budgeting process, the organization should ensure that the resource allocations currently reflected in the portfolio are aligned with the company's strategic goals. Also, all current activities should be reanalyzed for strategic fit. Sometimes you've got to kill a few sacred cows.

One devoted portfolio manager is Peter Thompson, general manager for integrated business solutions at BT Exact. BT Exact is the external services arm for British Telecommunications. Every level in BT Exact's portfolio is specifically identified. Each level has its own definition, metrics, and critical success factors. For example, the lowest level in the portfolio is made up of projects. *Projects* are defined as tactical activities. They are measured by cost and schedule. Successful projects are those that come in on time and on budget. A program is the next level up in the portfolio. A project must belong to a program. A program can be made up of several projects. A *program* is defined as strategic activity. Its metric is the delivery of business value. Its success criterion is that it must deliver business value. Each level in the portfolio adds something to the portfolio.

BT Exact's budget cycle is very labor intensive, says Thompson. Every year, the company reanalyzes all existing programs to see if they still make sense. BT Exact made the decision that in the telecommunications industry, where technology and peoples' tastes are changing rapidly, the company needed to ensure that all activities support its current strategic plan.

By integrating your portfolio management processes with your budgeting processes, you have the ability to look forward and identify future resource needs. If your company is asking you to spend more next year on new product development, that will usually translate into an increased need for R&D workers. Conversely, if your company is asking you to pull back on that and focus instead on cost reduction, you know you need more resources concentrating on those initiatives.

Opportunity Analysis

Once you know where you are in terms of your portfolio, *opportunity analysis* helps you figure out what, if anything, to add—and what must be dropped as a result.

Many times, opportunities are decided on the basis of decidedly unquantitative methods. The charisma of the sponsor, perhaps. Sometimes a manager will direct his or her people to work quietly on something new, and then present it as a "new" opportunity with the selling point that it's already half done. Other times, people are shamed into doing it and are labeled, "doesn't get it" if they question a sexy new initiative.

Just as misguided are organizations who go off the deep end using extremely sophisticated financial scoring systems to determine which opportunities to go after. This is the notorious *analysis paralysis problem*. We have seen a system that required 25 steps of analysis even before the initial approval. This system relied on dozens of attributes, including probability of commercial success, probability of technical success, benefit stream, cost stream, net present value, risks, time value of money, and so on. This system has a certain amount of engineering appeal, but even after you dig through all that computation, we feel that there is too much uncertainty in the figures to support such a rigorous analysis. It gives a false sense of certainty to an uncertain set of numbers.

In step 3, prioritizing your portfolio, we outlined some general rules about measuring both costs as well as benefits for existing programs. All of that applies to analyzing new opportunities as well. The most important thing to understand about opportunity analysis is that you are working with best guesses and educated forecasts. In the next chapter, we'll go step by step through the opportunity analysis process. To meet our purposes in this chapter, we will share some of our customers' thoughts on how far to go before jumping into a new program.

Typically, organizations are reluctant to accept opportunity management as a discipline, thinking that if it takes too long to analyze new opportunities, it will only serve to slow things down. But one of our customers, the IT organization for the headquarters of a large petrochemical company, which we will call Big Oil, has a simple yet effective opportunity analysis process. Big Oil IT has implemented opportunity management in a relatively painless manner. Big Oil IT does not rely on heavy financial analysis; instead, it concentrates on verifying that the program's sponsor has an adequate plan in place to address the business issues. Big Oil IT concentrates on emphasizing the simplicity of the data needed and the reasons for it.

"New opportunities only need a few data points," says the program manager at Big Oil IT. "Start date, end date, resources needed, and availability needed. There's no need for detailed resource requirements and schedules." In other words, you do not have to say that you need Jim between 2:00 and 3:00 in the morning on Wednesday.

The Big Oil IT program manager was able to show that even a fairly small amount of quantitative data can do a very good job in opportunity analysis. Simply asking these questions about start and end dates made the opportunity analysis work better. It improved people's estimating, and, as a result, program end dates became more and more realistic. Decisions would either be yes, no, or defer. If an opportunity were deferred, it would be used as an input to future capacity planning.

A slightly different approach to opportunity management is taken by the shared-services organization at a large retail chain; let's call this company Eponymous. The shared-services organization at Eponymous consists of the departments that support all of the different brands. It consists of the legal, finance, IT, and other groups. The shared-services organization must meet the needs of all of the brands at Eponymous. Each opportunity is first given a value statement, similar to a program charter. Then, each opportunity is analyzed for measurability and value.

The Eponymous shared-services organization then discusses how measurable an opportunity's benefits and costs may be. They try to quantify the risks of estimating future benefit streams. The further out in the future a benefit is forecast, the riskier, and hence less measurable, that benefit is. Similarly, costs are analyzed for measurability. They ask, "Have we ever done this before? Is this similar in scope and size to other activities we know we can do? Do we have the required new skills to handle this new opportunity?" The less measurable an opportunity's benefits and costs are, the more risky it is.

After they have discussed the measurability of the opportunity, only then do they concentrate on the actual values of the benefits and the costs. They detail the benefit; they define purchase costs, labor costs, leases, and anything else that adds cost. They define the expected timing of both their cost outlays as well as their benefits streams. This process is outlined in Figure 5–4.

And here's the hammer hanging over the exercise: To discourage managers from being overly optimistic with cost-savings estimates for pet projects, any potential cost reductions for new opportunities automatically get rolled into budget savings for the next year. In this way, the budget gets reduced if the opportunity is funded. You say a new order process will lower overtime labor costs at the end of the month? Tremendous— your funding begins with the cost savings you stipulate. The manager must receive the benefit he or she expects. This is a fairly harsh rule, but one that the people at Eponymous think keeps everyone very truthful.

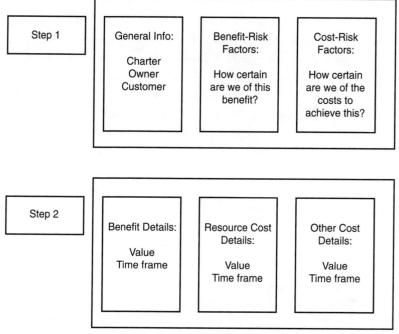

Figure 5–4

Checklist for Managing a Portfolio
- Have you reviewed your portfolio in conjunction with the budgeting process?
- Are resource allocations aligned with your company's strategic goals?
- Are all current activities reassessed during the budgeting process?
- Can you achieve your objectives with your budgeted resources within a reasonable time frame?
- Are new opportunities analyzed to see where they fit into your current portfolio?
- Are new opportunities analyzed using both cost as well as benefit information?

The Payoff

Most organizations begin more opportunities than they have the capacity to complete. As a result, there is always too much to do and not enough time to do it. Teams are starved of needed resources, or disrupted by knowledge workers being pulled to provide emergency staffing on a hot new program. Proper portfolio and opportunity management will give knowledge managers the ability to assign their resources to the right initiatives. It will allow managers to anticipate future demands on their knowledge workers as their initiatives progress through their life cycle. They will be able to forecast the effects of redeploying workers to different initiatives. They will be able to take a look at the opportunities of developing new initiatives to achieve a maximum return on their resources.

A portfolio also solves another problem: the information vacuum. Executives define strategic initiatives, but if they lack a feedback mechanism to verify implementation and effectiveness, they end up practicing "*I Dream of Jeannie* Initiative Management." Portfolio management provides that feedback mechanism. It provides access to information to the right people at the right level of detail. In the next chapter, we'll go into the step by steps of the actual opportunity analysis process.

Table 5–5 summarizes the six different steps you should take in portfolio management, as well as the benefits to be derived at each step.

Table 5–5: Benefits for Each Step in Portfolio Management

Step	Action	Benefit	Analytics
First	Define	Communicates priorities Provides framework for accountability	Historical
Second	Review	Highlights redundant priorities Highlights unneeded priorities	Historical
Third	Prioritize	Forces alignment Allows the analysis of tradeoffs	Real time
Fourth	Categorize	Gains strategic focus	Real time
Fifth	Balance	Balances the work Achieves strategic balances	Predictive
Sixth	Manage	Integrates with budgeting–strategy setting process Allows opportunity analysis	Predictive

Figuring Out How to Do It Right Every Time

This chapter discusses process as the key to any effective, longlasting organization. Process is a tactical fundamental, and it should be a preoccupation and priority at the company's operational level.

DAVID RASPALLO IS A CALM, direct, no-nonsense kind of guy. He is the chief information officer at Textron Financial, a subsidiary of Textron Industries, a Providence, Rhode Island, company with 71,000 employees and businesses in a number of fascinating but radically different sorts of industries, including aircraft (they make Bell helicopters and Cessna airplanes), real estate, golf carts, and a finance organization with $9 billion in assets.

Textron's activities range from one-transaction-at-a-time–oriented financial services that are conducted almost entirely by knowledge workers, to pure manufacturing operations where workers take "a hunk of aluminum and build a $15 million plane out of it," as Raspallo puts it. Textron has enjoyed increased revenues and earnings continuously for 23 straight years. This management team clearly knows how to run complex businesses well.

When earnings are plunging and market share is eroding, just about anybody can see an opportunity for improvement. But Textron realized, despite the soothing balm of its earnings steadily rising, that it could do better in terms of operating costs. To Raspallo and Textron's top executives, attacking those numbers meant focusing particularly hard on company processes.

To many knowledge workers, process smells of bean counting and bureaucrats, of nerdy, operationally inexperienced systems consultants who cash a paycheck based on finding something wrong with everybody's system, no matter how good it is. Raspallo experienced just such resistance when he began to talk about creating replicable processes across his different organizations. His workers asked rather incredulously, How in the world could we, who have already mastered this, possibly perform this task in any way other than the way we do? And among the questions with which some top executives needled him: "So, you're going for ISO 9000 so that you can prove to everyone just how wonderful you are?"

Raspallo held his course. He patiently explained to his workers that there's almost no process anywhere that can't be improved upon if you study it. Second, he discussed the notion he calls "tribal knowledge," or the oral traditions of training people to understand how and why something is done. Tribal knowledge degrades, Raspallo explains. "It may very well be that Mary is absolutely the most efficient, excellent person possible to carry on a given task, but someday that task will have to be completed when Mary is sick or she retires. However good she is at that task, she may or may not be a very good teacher of that task, and she may not even perceive it to be in her best interest to teach anyone to understand and complete it the way she can. If you have a number of projects that rely on specialized knowledge that is locked inside specific individuals, you are in trouble."

CIOs like Raspallo tend to be very good at understanding the value of process. They are constantly coming up against the nightmares created by disparate systems and standards inside an organization that prevent data from being exchanged efficiently. Unfortunately, they are sometimes alone in that understanding. In this case, however, Raspallo found two allies: First, the president of Textron Financial happened to take a project management course and emerged a convert to the power of process. Second, the CEO of the company listened carefully to Raspallo's case and was willing to give it his personal endorsement. "You need to have a CEO who listens to all the complaining and is able to say, 'I hear what you're saying, I understand where you're coming from, but it's so important for us to improve and get better, we are going to attack this," Raspallo says.

He was also aided in more widespread attention to process issues by some dramatic, singular successes that his efforts yielded. One interesting example is the closing of loans to golf course operators, a very specialized financial service that one of Textron's companies provided. Before Raspallo and his team attacked the existing process, studied it, and worked with the team to revamp it, it took 90 days for the average loan to close, from opening the request or inquiry to the money arriving. The folks doing it thought they had it down pat and that most of the delays they encountered were special circumstances related to a given deal that no process could maneuver around.

After the process revamping, the average time fell to 45 days.

This story gets Rhonda's Process Queen heart beating like a hummingbird's. There are lonelier jobs than process evangelist—but not many. Process is at the heart of a sustainable enterprise. But some people just naturally employ process-based thinking, and some people do not. Whether learned or genetic, this split is real. Rhonda was trained as a nuclear engineer and can't imagine approaching life and business with anything other than a process orientation (a source of comfort for those who live near nuclear power plants). Farzad, on the other hand, is a true entrepreneur, an eternal optimist who is more inclined to believe that enthusiasm and leadership can overcome anything.

It took the software equivalent of a miracle to convert Farzad to the process camp: We started Niku, which makes software tools for integrated program and knowledge management within organizations, back in 1998. We had big dreams that we were impatient to accomplish. We knew we were going to grow fast. At the end of the first year, the development organization was 30 people. At the end of the second year, our development organization was 100 people. And at the end of the third year, we had over 300 people. We were growing so fast that it was essential to have a strong process.

The problem today is that knowledge workers tend to think that process is for later or they don't have time to read about it and implement it as a new tool. As we struggled to develop our process, Farzad looked at Rhonda's development organization and worried aloud: "We need to get something out! We aren't coding!" The process definition period also was not terribly popular with the troops. We had a conversation with our director of development, in which we showed him a draft of a process flowchart. He asked me, "Who is going to enforce this?" His look told me it was certainly not him.

Rhonda knew she was right about process. She had used process in her 20 years of professional experience, which included everything from installing emergency response systems in nuclear power plants to setting up quality teams at Oracle.

When we were setting up development processes at Niku, Rhonda told her team: "If you're working, and there is some confusion as to who should do something or how it should be done, stop everything and figure it out." She has consulted for a number of manufacturing companies and firmly believes lots of practices from that arena apply to the knowledge workplace—such as the line stoppages that we used in the 1980s as we converted manufacturing operations to just-in-time systems. We now insist that whenever we find problems, we solve them before moving on.

The upshot of enforcing these processes is that we made our targets. Our first release was on time to the day. As were our second and third releases. We were able to deliver our fourth release, a full suite of products, in 9 months. If you know much about software development you know that making your completion target is a miracle. We think our religious devotion to process made that miracle happen.

This is a good example of a healthy check-and-balance situation in the knowledge workplace. You can't go so overboard with process that people become discouraged and bogged down in reporting and detail. CEOs get bored and frustrated with excessive process. They do not want the minute details on everything. They do want people to demonstrate good judgment and report progress, problems, and data the CEOs need to know to make good decisions. CEOs have to deal with the big picture. As you'll see in Chapter 9, you will come to appreciate that you need high-level leadership and vision, plus those process evangelists, to keep an organization balanced in its most productive zone—midway between irrational exuberance and oppressive bureaucracy.

In the late 1990s, it was epidemic to discard classic management principles like process because of the exaggerated perceived need for speed. In 1999 there was a sign on a wall in a now-defunct dot.com that read: "Ready Fire Aim." In the not-so-long-ago old days, that would have been a hand-lettered sign some malcontent posted to make fun of a dumb manager. In this outfit, the misguided CEO loved the sign so much he had it printed up, and he posted it all over the place.

Using the Accountability Management System to Attack Process

At this stage, you've begun to attack the tactical elements of your job by taking a hard look at your portfolio, determining whether what your people are working on is closely aligned with your corporate goals, and gaining visibility at the program level. Now that you are doing the right things, you can concentrate on doing them right. Process is the key to repeatable success.

Broadly speaking, process management in the workplace is the definition of roles and responsibilities for any activity:

- Who is ultimately responsible?
- What is the time frame for completion?
- What are the resources needed for completion?
- What is the sequence of steps to be completed, and the rules governing the steps?
- What are the tangible, reportable milestones?
- What is the outcome and the deadline for the outcome you're seeking?

If you do nothing else but religiously ask those questions, you will be ahead of the pack. It is astounding how much work gets launched with unclear objectives, fuzzy reporting lines, uncertain or nonexistent deadlines, no budget for what resources the work will require, and no requirement that the team is accountable on a regular basis for hitting milestones. How many times do you hear otherwise intelligent and valuable knowledge workers justify some effort by telling you: "It didn't cost us anything—we did it ourselves!" Every minute of every workday has both a real overhead dollar cost and an opportunity cost to the company. The time we waste fumbling around on something disorganized and ill-defined, or the time we spend redoing something done poorly because there was inadequate coordination of efforts, is time we can't spend on a killer product that will have customers lining up.

So take a minute to think about an activity that's important to you and see if you can answer all those questions we just listed. Don't fudge. Don't let yourself off the hook by convincing yourself that yours is such an unusual and special situation that these questions don't apply. If you can't answer all those questions for all activities in your portfolio, then swallow hard and pay attention. As you'll soon see, it's not difficult to organize your workplace so that gathering that information becomes automatic.

One of the ironies of process is that while some say it can sap energy from creative people, in fact, not addressing the seemingly trivial issues early on creates obstacles that really do sap energy and create frustration and waste. If you were to position a chair between your bed and the bathroom, every morning when you got up you would have to walk around the chair to avoid stumbling into it. Some process scofflaw stuck that chair there without thinking. The process police scream: Move the chair! The longer you wait to move it, the more you prolong the inefficiency, the more often you stub your toe. As you come to appreciate process, you will find chairs all over your company standing between teams, between people and resources, and between systems. Move those chairs!

Types of Processes

In certain industries, such as large capital equipment manufacturing, there are professionals who spend their entire lives as process wonks, endlessly debating where to allocate indirect costs. When you're running extraordinarily complex programs like the construction of an airplane, coordinating and monitoring process can make the difference between success and failure on a huge scale. Despite the warm feelings Rhonda has for those so inclined, however, in the knowledge workplace, process wonks operate best as a secret society that actually makes an effort to speak English to civilians.

So, let's start by simplifying views of managing process issues. There are two types of process a manager of knowledge workers needs to be clear about: project management processes and business processes.

A *project management process* describes how activities are created, planned, performed, controlled, and completed. It exists to ensure that information is available to management and executives to provide them visibility so that they can verify that work is progressing correctly. There are different kinds of project management approaches, but all of them require that you be consistent in managing your activities.

A *business process* describes how your organization does what it does. If you are a marketing organization, your business processes are marketing processes—creating a press release, creating an ad campaign, or putting on a seminar for prospects, for example. If you are a legal department, you may have a special process for developing and finalizing contracts that involves a series of document review checks for red flags and key provisions, feedback to all parties, and document formalizing. Business processes describe your organization's version of best practices for adding value. Typically, business processes are embedded in the planning phase of the project management process, and then worked in the performing phase, as I'll explain in a moment.

This distinction, between project management processes and business processes, is crucial, because the type of process tells a knowledge manager when to control his or her knowledge workers tightly or loosely. Knowledge managers should implement controls in a project management process to gain visibility while allowing their knowledge workers the freedom to do their jobs creatively, efficiently, and effectively. Some key differences between these two types of processes are shown in Table 6–1.

The Project Management Process

There are many types of project management process systems available for use in organizations today. Some professional organizations both in

Table 6-1: Differences between Project Management Processes and Business Processes

	Project Management Processes	Business Processes
Purpose	Provide management visibility	Provide guidance and best practices
Key audience	Management and executives	Knowledge workers
Required?	Emphatically *yes*, all steps cast in stone	No, depends on the type of work
Better known as . . .	Overhead, bureaucracy, management BS (unfortunately)	Best practices, guidelines, rules of thumb
Defined by	Project management gurus	The knowledge workers themselves
Owned by	Management	Knowledge workers
Benefits	Visibility	Efficiency
Applicability	Broad and similar for all types of organizations	Specific to each industry and even to each organization

the United States and abroad market their own proprietary project management processes. The most popular resource, at least in the United States, is the Project Management Institute (PMI). Others that are widely used and adapted include the Plan/Do/Check/Act (PDCA) Productivity Cycle popularized by the American Productivity and Quality Center (APQC). Many others exist.[1]

From our own experience and discussions with scores of companies, it seems clear that the most effective processes are the ones that encompass five key phases: initiation, planning, performing, correcting, and closing, as shown in Figure 6–1.

The first phase of project management overlaps with opportunity analysis from Chapter 5.

Remember that what we are advocating here is a systematic, consistent approach to the management of all your activities. You're not going to be lax with one team because you feel its leader has special mojo and you trust her to bring everything in on time, or remind another team in which you have less faith that Big Brother is watching. This is about visibility and having a good handle on what we're doing and where everyone is.

Five Phases of a Good Project Management Process

Phase I. Initiation

Set rules and parameters for suggesting new activities. Fully describe the activities, and then ruthlessly embrace or reject them.

In the last chapter we developed a framework that describes the important activities for an organization—the portfolio. The most critical task in the first phase of project management is to analyze a new opportunity and discern whether or not it fits in the portfolio. Opportunities are created from a variety of sources—customers, management, your employees. Regardless of the source, all ideas for new activities

Figure 6–1

should be put through the same process since the analysis performed in this phase is crucial for some downstream steps. This is how we get rid of *I Dream of Jeannie* management.

Whoever proposes a new opportunity needs to do a little work to clearly define the problem or situation and suggest a solution or improvement. Then that person puts forth the opportunity for management to review. The review requires management involvement and, if the expected cost is over a certain preset amount, the opportunity may also require upper-level executive review and approval. This phase is shown in Figure 6–2.

The initiation phase can be short or long depending upon your business and the specific opportunity. In the knowledge marketplace, some program initiation phases take months. If this is true in your company, and you find that you are spending a significant amount of resources on determining whether or not to pursue an opportunity, set up some minimal criteria opportunities must meet to even be considered candidates for initiation.

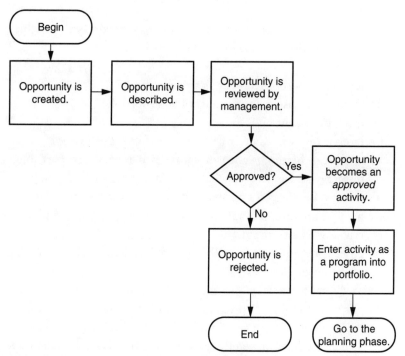

Figure 6–2

For example, Fred Jewell, an associate partner at Accenture, had a client who made a lot of enhancement requests to Accenture, which was providing IT services to the company on an ongoing basis. For example, the customer would ask for enhancement A. Accenture would develop a proposal and respond that enhancement A would take 6 weeks and cost a certain amount. The customer would then say, "Great! Can you fit in enhancement B as well?" Accenture would go back, spend a lot of time rescoping, and give the customer the answer: "A + B will take 22 weeks." Then the customer would say: "Ouch, that's way too much. Please just do A."

The scoping and rescoping efforts would sometimes take up to 80 percent of the total time to implement the enhancement. Jewell's organization and his client were losing time and money by repeating these scenarios, so they worked out a new process where enhancements are explored together in real time rather than through multiple hand-offs.

The following checklist includes issues management needs to consider about proposed opportunities:

- Has the new opportunity been fully described? Is it valuable? Are both costs and estimated benefits believable? Are they well considered?
- Does it fit into the company's strategic goals?
- Does it increase the total value of your portfolio?
- Is it within your budget?
- Does it result in a better balanced portfolio? For example, will it provide a better balance of short-term revenues versus long-term revenues? Are you balancing the needs of all your customers, or are you concentrating on only one sector? Do you have a mixture of high-risk–high-return programs and low-risk–low-return programs?
- Does it require resources the company is comfortable allocating to the program?
- What has to move out in order to take on this program, and is it a fair swap? Does this program score higher than one you will be moving out? Or can you do it right now?
- When you have moved things around to fit this in, does the value of your portfolio increase?

If management can answer yes to the checklist questions, the opportunity should be approved. Then management should give the project to an owner, put it in the portfolio, and move it into the next phase: planning. If no, management needs to do some more balancing of this opportunity against the current programs in its portfolio, rethink the approach, or drop it.

Phase 2. Planning

Set a budget and identify milestones.

Once an activity successfully passes through the initiation phase, it becomes a program in your portfolio. You then enter the planning phase to outline the steps to take, allocate the resources required, and refine the initial estimates. The program owner should be responsible for the planning phase.

Choose your program steps and their expected completion schedule carefully since you will judge progress based on making or missing those dates. The dates for completing the steps are also the points in the program where you gain visibility. These steps should be tied to customer approvals. Have your customer, or someone close to your customer, verify that progress has been achieved. It is easy, when time is tight, to fool yourself that something has occurred when it really hasn't—such as "finish final draft." Who really decides when it is finished? Is that person the right authority for this check? Or might that person be so invested in getting this step completed that his or her judgment could be compromised if things got a bit dicey?

A more effective milestone might be: "Customer approves final draft." (We are going to discuss the business processes that are embedded in the planning step and its milestones after we finish discussing the project management process.)

Each step has a time frame—that is how long the step is expected to take. The time it takes to complete a program will depend on each step's time frame and the sequence in which the steps are performed. Steps can be taken serially or in parallel.

Next, identify the resources needed for each step in the plan. Make sure that the team has enough extra capacity to work on these things. You should know how the team's personnel are deployed on its projects because you are tracking these activities in your portfolio. Get buy-in for these personnel resources by getting their or their manager's commitment, and lock down their schedules. Then define the deliverables that are required for each phase or step in the process. For knowledge work, these are usually the only physically definable actions that signal "done." They also serve as an artifact for future use. What is actually completed? A draft document? A presentation? A bound report? Deliverables are a way of verifying that a step was completed. Contrast the following: "Think hard about what to say to the judge" versus "File motion." Which attorney would you hire?

Once all steps, resources, and deliverables have been identified, the original estimates for costs and benefits should be revisited. If either of these attributes have changed significantly, by more than 10 percent, the program should go back through the initiation phase to verify whether the company still wants to do this project. Does it still make sense? This step is very important because initial assumptions may have shifted significantly during the flight, and opening the overhead bin may result in your getting bonked on the head with a larger-than-expected program cost. This step is the first of many replanning steps that will be the key to achieving visibility during the next phase.

You emerge from the planning phase with your initial plan; this includes both a schedule and a budget. This is your baseline. Your baseline does not change for the life of the program. You will constantly refer back to the baseline to make sure you are making progress and staying within your budget. The planning phase is summarized in Figure 6–3 and the following checklist.

Checklist for the Planning Phase
- Is the owner, that is, the person who is responsible for delivering this piece of work identified?
- Is the program manager, the person who is responsible for guiding the progress of this work (can be the owner) identified?

Schedule
- Do you have a schedule?
- Does the schedule break down the work into small enough steps so that you have visibility on progress?

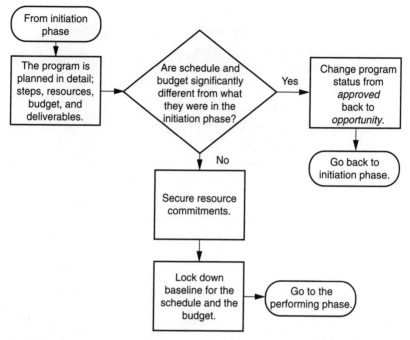

Figure 6–3

- Are customers used to verify progress?
- Are deliverables, their timing and type, identified in the schedule?
- Is the schedule baselined?

Budget
- Do you have a budget?
- Does the budget coincide with the schedule?
- Does it clearly state the timing of costs incurred?
- Are costs adequately categorized (materials, labor, capital expenses, travel, consulting, fees, and so on) so that you have visibility on spending?
- Is the budget baselined?

Resources
- Are resources aligned with the schedule?
- Have all needed resources been identified?
- Have explicit resource commitments been made and explicitly approved?

Approval
- Are the planned schedule and budget estimates within 10 percent of the initiation phase estimates?

Phase 3. Performing

Demand accurate, current data.

Tell your people: Do what the plan says. Do it according to the plan. On a weekly basis, ask for status reports detailing progress down to the step level. Ask your people how much time they spent on the step during the preceding week and how much more time they need to spend to complete the step. Ask for updates on cost, too. How much have they spent? How much more will they spend before the step is completed?

The forecasted schedule and budget information should be compared with the baseline data on a weekly basis (see Figure 6–4). Replan

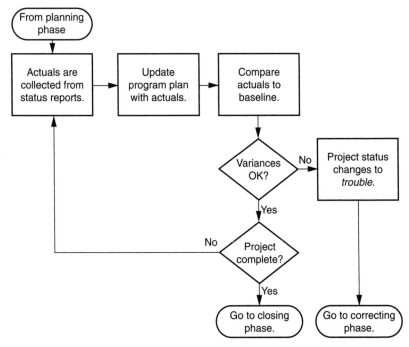

Figure 6–4

and reforecast on a weekly basis. Management should jump in if the forecasted numbers start to deviate significantly from the baseline.

Use your status reports and weekly meetings with your knowledge workers to keep yourself on track. Expand your status reports so that it's easy for you to gain visibility, see progress, and identify problems. Table 6–2 shows the format for your own status reports.

This constant replanning is what our colleague Terry Ash, project manager for the E-Solutions Division of Hewlett-Packard, calls *closed-loop project control*. Closed-loop project control is your ticket to visibility nirvana. You control your projects so that there's constant feedback to ensure that every piece of information is always up to date. That way, you don't get bad news at the end of a project. Instead you get information continuously, and you can make small adjustments along the way—as necessary.

In other words, closed-loop project control is the opposite of what often occurs today—static rather than real-time project planning. For instance, one of the traditional tools of the project manager is the Gantt chart. Designed at the beginning of a project to allocate various resources, this plan is often neglected and even forgotten once it has been distributed. It is the illusion of a plan because it is rarely updated

Table 6-2: Status Reports

Programs	Progress	Plans	Problems
Program name	Note what the baseline schedule says should have been completed this week, compare this to the actual steps accomplished.	Note what the baseline schedule says should be completed next week. Compare this to the current forecast for whether it can be accomplished.	Any schedule variance over 10%
	Note the baseline costs that should have been incurred this week. Compare these to the actual costs incurred.	Note the baseline cost that should be incurred next week. Compare to the current forecast for whether it will be on track.	Any schedule variance over 10%

to accommodate the ebb and flow of resources. With increasing financial and competitive pressure in today's market, it is essential that the right information is accessible at all times and, for this to happen, companies must look to always-on technology.

The constant replanning forces the manager to confront problems as they occur. It also tends to expose weaknesses in the original plan. Rather than burying them until there is no choice but to confront them, weaknesses are reviewed every week. Curveballs may appear, and assumptions may be proven wrong. When that occurs: Fix the plan, don't just change the chart.

This constant introspection may not be fun, but it is a whole lot more fun than never knowing what your true progress is. This frequent feedback leads to greater visibility.

Simply comparing baselines to forecasts is sufficient to manage a majority of programs. If you need even more control, however, you can use the concept of *earned value analysis* (EVA) as a measure to determine progress.[2] This is a very robust method of measuring progress on your projects. It was originally used to value work-in-process inventories for manufacturing companies. Using this method, variances are expressed based on two measurements: the *budgeted cost of work scheduled* (BCWS) and the *actual cost of work performed* (ACWP). The BCWS represents the plan that is to be followed, and it is the standard. It is calculated based on the number of hours people are expected to work times their pay rates, including overhead. This figure is compared to the ACWP, the amount of money actually spent doing the work. Comparing standards to actuals yields a variance. Both usage and cost variance components are analyzed.

Checklist for the Performing Phase
- Are you measuring your progress and updating your plan constantly?
- Are baseline versus actual schedules and budgets communicated weekly? Are the program's total schedule and budget forecasted weekly?
- Are you making sure you don't shoot the messengers when they unearth problems in the plan? You want the problems laid out on the table when there's still time to fix them.

Phase 4. Correcting

Monitor the plan for signs of trouble and fix the trouble first

Bad news looms on the horizon. Knowledge workers hear the distant wail of a tornado siren and swing into emergency mode. Priority 1: Soften up management so that management will be more receptive to the bad news. When asked how things are going, start to grimace just a tad and say "It's a stretch goal. . . . It's tight. . . . My part is going fine, but I'm really worried about Jack. . . ." Crisis-driven knowledge workers delay or duck out of all reporting situations. They barricade themselves into their cubes, thinking, If we work really, really hard for the next 18 hours, ignoring needs for both food and bathroom breaks, and don't talk to anyone, we'll get this puppy back on track. Fear spreads. Clusters of managers gather around the knowledge workers, all telling them to work faster.

An old friend of ours calls this behavior "charging on, unimpeded by progress." Once a program is deemed in need of correction, it should be flagged as a "trouble" program. Getting the program out of trouble status is more important than working on the program. The team is probably too close to the program and the trouble to get themselves out of it. They need objectivity to help them make good decisions.

Figure 6–5 shows the steps in the correcting phase. If you have a baselined budget and schedule, you can get good, hard facts. Take a look at the budget variance. Take a look also at the effort variance. If either of these variance numbers are greater than 10 percent, you are in trouble. This is your big, red, flashing light. This is the scratchy voice over the loudspeaker that orders you to "Stop and get out of the car."

You're out of the car. You do not have the right to remain silent. Here are your options:

- You can revisit the original program charter. Refamiliarize yourself and the team with what you are really trying to accomplish. Is everything in the plan essential for delivering on the charter?
- You can reallocate resources, adding or shifting resources from different parts of the organization. Take a look in your portfolio and look at other lower-value programs. See if you can move some resources from those programs to the trouble program. Look to add more experienced people; look to add more people.

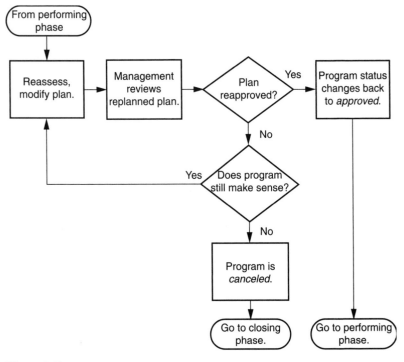

Figure 6–5

- You can review dependencies on other programs: Are other trouble programs making this one late? Can you shift resources upstream and bring in the late prerequisite programs earlier? Is this the program that is gumming up the whole works? Can you shift some work around to deliver smaller but more important elements earlier?
- You can restructure the work to get around bottlenecks: Break one activity into two, rethink a later step, and so on.
- You can try to adjust your scope: Were you trying to bite off too much? Can you get rid of some bells and whistles? Can you deliver the same solution, only in a different way? Are any steps unnecessary or unnecessarily detailed? Can you deliver less?
- You can adjust your deliverables: Was a 300-page report overkill? Will 30 do?
- You can try to reset expectations, either on the part of the customer, your management, or whoever will derive the benefit. Try to renegotiate the purpose of the program or its outcome.

Without this kind of visibility and the attendant fine-tuning, your choices for dealing with trouble programs are usually more limited: continue or cancel. Instead of just flipping an on-off switch for your knowledge workers when things get hairy, with a good project management process, you can confidently make minor adjustments. This is the power of visibility.

Phase 5. Close

Be honest. Learn from what's happened before you close the books.

This step, depicted in Figure 6–6, exists to keep you honest. How did you really do? Did it truly take 6 months to accomplish something, or did you use pee-wee golf rules and stop counting strokes (months) after 8? Did it really cost $57,000? Or did you just stop comparing the budget to the original plan?

A truly great organization will use end data to verify that its processes are good. If not, they improve them. If you standardize a project management process, everyone can use it. If it works, then your success is repeatable! If it doesn't, then you can improve it. As Richard Whelchel, of Coca-Cola Bottling Co. says, "This is the way out of the bog."

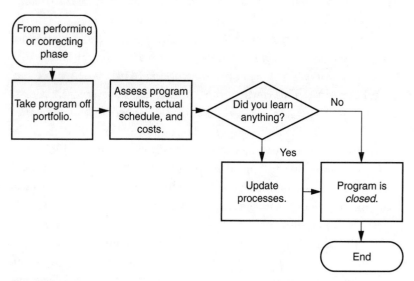

Figure 6–6

If the program was a success, that is, if it came in on time, it was on budget, and it delivered on its charter, very little needs to be done in the step. But if it could have been improved, talk about it. Just make sure it doesn't turn into a witch-hunt. Focus on the problem, not the people. If something went wrong, ask "Why did it happen?" at least three times. Figure out the reason things went astray. Then you should develop a response that prevents the situation from recurring. Train people to do it the new way.

Rhonda once worked for someone on a program that was 18 months late, 1 month at a time. Each month, for 18 months, she had to go to key customers and tell them that it would be just 1 more month before the program was completed. After the third time delivering this message, the conversations weren't very fun. This was the experience that turned us into process wonks. We hope that no one ever has to go through something like that. When Rhonda asked one of the directors that she worked with—let's call him C. L. Ueless—what we should do on the next program to make sure it wouldn't be so bad, he replied, "We will just have to do better." There was no correcting step midway or at any time during our perpetually late effort. Our organization floundered like a drowning person, unable to reach the life raft while our managers leaned over the edge of the boat, saying, in effect, "Flounder harder." And when it was all over, they decided that we just hadn't floundered hard enough and should try to do so next time.

This closing phase allows you to implement a process of continuous improvement in your organization. Learn from your mistakes. Your knowledge workers will thank you for working to make them more successful next time. This is where the continuous-improvement, process-oriented *Six Sigma Methodology* comes in. Developed by Motorola, Inc., in the late 1980s, Six Sigma uses statistical information about processes "to increase customer satisfaction, maximize process efficiencies, increase competitive advantage and market share," and decrease operating expenses (mu.motorola.com). The basic idea is to evaluate a business process such that the company identifies the desired result, measures deviations from that desired result, and revises the process to reduce the deviations from the result. The new result is then measured to see if the change had the desired effect. Applying this evaluation consistently heightens customer satisfaction, decreases product defects, and decreases cycle times.

Six Sigma is a statistical term, meaning a very small number of errors. In order to get Six Sigma quality, a process must yield no more than 3.4 errors out of every million tries. That's a pretty lofty goal, but some companies are achieving it. Its proponents say that it saves them millions, if not billions, every year and that it results in a consistently excellent customer experience. No matter what the size of your company, applying Six Sigma principles can improve its processes.

Finally, be sure to celebrate the close of every program. You and your employees learn from both successes and failures.

Business Process

Project management processes are so important that we consider them sacred. Thou shalt not change these steps. However, the other type of process, the business process, must be a lot more flexible. This is how you institutionalize best practices and make sure your people are all working smart. It allows you to give your people the flexibility to attack knowledge problems by themselves.

When knowledge workers balk at process, it is typically because the wrong things get carved in stone. Some manager takes a process that works well in one situation and decrees that people will use it in another. The employees don't feel as though they own the process. They don't feel they have a say. Even if it's a good one, the inflexibility of the manager imposing it turns them off. And this approach doesn't inspire them to use their own brain cells to improve upon the process by applying their own synthesis of what they know and what's worked or not worked in the past. When a company is struggling with process, often it is because business processes are enforced like project management processes. What should be guidelines end up as rules. Whenever we have tried to dictate business processes, there's been pushback. Business processes must be owned by the people who do the work, and a manager must be open to those workers' input in adapting and improving those processes.

Business processes are designed to make sure people work and play well with others. Business processes in the knowledge workplace are not about spelling out every minute of an individual's day (Arrive in cubicle. Turn on computer. Log on, changing password if prompted to do so. Check e-mail. Respond only to messages from key team members or upper management. Get a cup of coffee, but only use milk if you've contributed your $5 to the quarterly milk budget . . .).

In a very small organization, it's sufficient to convey many simple business processes verbally. But remember Dave Raspallo's concerns about "tribal knowledge." The problem occurs as the tribe expands and the organization becomes increasingly dependent on a few medicine men to run things. Those people, in turn, may not see it as being in their own best interest to share their knowledge, or they may simply not perceive themselves to have time to share best practices. That's when inefficiencies run amok. You can't improve processes locked inside somebody's head. Best practices erode as people informally train each other and leave steps out. You create a culture that is unreceptive to accountability because everything's been handled so ad hoc.

Within reason, your knowledge workers should be given the freedom to consider a business process, take what they think is applicable for their own particular situation, and throw the rest away. Give them the freedom and flexibility to do their job, to solve a problem, to deal with an issue, to get something done. Whoa, you're thinking, What happened to adults being in charge?

Well, these are not contradictory notions if you're practicing accountability management. When the program itself is being carefully and closely watched, workers can be given the freedom to develop their own processes and improve upon those processes.

An effective coach provides the discipline framework: You shall attend practice; you shall agree to our conditioning program; you shall learn our playbook; you shall watch films of our opponents. In short, the mechanics of being on the team, which apply to every player, are enforced on a daily basis. Attendance is not optional. But coaches realize that the best athletes require some freedom, whether in how they prepare for the game or even in how they improvise when the game is underway. If the play says go right and there's nothing open on the right, the great athlete weighs the option and then goes left, and the coach applauds that maneuver. It was what the situation called for. The player had the basic skill and conditioning, he understood the goal, he realized the existing plan wouldn't achieve it, and so he used good, educated judgment and found another way. John Madden was a great coach because he could take players who had great talent but couldn't get along in highly structured, rigid systems. He respected those players, he organized them, but he also set them free to use their talents.

To succeed in the bulk of knowledge work situations that require flexibility and initiative, employees need the freedom to go left or right when conditions demand it. You can give them that freedom if, when the play is over, they have to report back to the huddle and be accountable for what they did, and also to face the coach.

So, the two types of process are distinct but complementary. Project management processes provide a framework for everyone to become aware of the real-time status of all activities. As such, there should be no exceptions or variations as to how the programs are initiated, planned, performed, corrected, and closed. Make no mistake: There needs to be real discipline in your organization in order to implement this. Business processes, on the other hand, are guidelines and best practices that should be consulted, analyzed, and potentially used depending upon the specifics of each situation. Frankly, these are more important than project management processes, and they become the steps that you define during the planning phase of project management.

Even though Rhonda is a dictator about project management, she's like the Dalai Lama when it comes to business processes. Business processes are more important to your ultimate success because they embody what you do. You have got to create a climate that embraces and builds upon processes. They need to be defined, understood, and communicated. This is how organizations learn and get better at whatever it is they do.

Happily, the way to define, understand, and communicate these processes is to make your knowledge workers responsible for them. All of your knowledge workers have something to add, something to contribute. We will revisit the issue in Chapter 8, when we discuss how to encourage the sharing of tacit knowledge. Your business processes are their way of adding to the total knowledge of your organization. In a sense, they can sign their work by authoring a process or a set of process steps.

Business Process Priorities

In evaluating your business processes, there are two areas you should address. First, there are basic activities any business faces that represent threats to your viability. Those demand specific, explicit processes for legal, financial, and customer-facing activities. For any business bigger than a handful of people, you need explicit processes for activities that involve intellectual property, contracts, or leases; you need to establish financial controls and signing authority for new hires and purchase orders; and you need some kind of process for customer-facing activities such as negotiating deals, making sales calls, or handling inquiries or complaints. These often boil down to very simple directives such as: Nobody can alter an employment offer in any way without approval from legal and the CEO; all lease agreements must be approved by both legal and finance before submitting to the COO; all customer complaints will first be vetted by the marketing department. Allow people to mess with this stuff creatively and you could be out of business.

We process wonks have a saying: Every problem is a process problem. That means every snag or curveball is typically a chance to examine some element of an existing process for gaps. When Rhonda ran the development operations at Niku, the organization had to buy some tools for software development. One developer decided that he really wanted a very fancy, top-of-the-line tool, and he spoke with someone in the business development group who immediately ran off and signed an agreement to get the developer the tool. Rhonda never signed off on this. His boss or Rhonda could have set the young developer straight that this tool was way too powerful and complex for what we were doing—but neither were consulted. The business development chief had signing authority, but it wasn't attended by any sort of process to review such a major capital outlay. So, we were the proud parents of a bouncing baby $25,000 code tool that, for the kind of work we were doing, was like buying a Cray supercomputer to balance your checkbook. It's sitting on a shelf. We put explicit signing authority processes in place and undoubtedly have saved considerable money in the wake of this one expensive fiasco.

The second area ripe for looking at business processes is much more fun and has much higher potential to achieve your business goals.

Look at those activities that are the core of your business. Target those activities that generate revenue or add the most to your contribution margin (revenue minus variable costs), or that deal with your bread and butter. Identify the things that, given a 10 percent improvement, could yield the biggest improvement in results. Do not waste your time on low-priority activities or low-margin activities. If your organization could do just one thing better, what would it be? Start with that.

Let's play with this example. You run a greeting card business. Sales have been sagging. You need to revitalize the design of your greeting cards to attract more sales.

You start by asking your design manager for the business process your design team utilizes to design cards. You've never dictated a process to him because things have gone well until quite recently. He comes back with this:

> **Hold meeting of creative staff and discuss ideas → Decide on 20 new cards per quarter → Designers provide sketches of those cards → Design manager approves and reviews with vice president of marketing → Design is forwarded to production.**

Very good. A logical process. But when you discussed how to improve the quality of the cards, the design manager looked at you blankly and said you can't dictate creativity. He'll encourage his team to try harder, but he thinks the salespeople just aren't properly marketing the very excellent cards his group produces.

Next you huddle with your management team to figure out how to raise the metabolism of the design group so they are putting out better cards that will drive sales. This is a classic knowledge worker problem: How do you raise the level of a creativity-based, unquantifiable activity?

"Tell them to design harder," offers C. L. Ueless, unhelpfully.

"Hire Mike Magic from our biggest competitor. I know he wants four times as much as we pay anyone, but he's got the special sauce when it comes to greeting cards," says the head of human resources.

"Listen to our sales staff," sighs Sam, the vice president of sales.

"Huh? Elaborate on that, Sam."

"Our retailers have been screaming for more traditional, reassuring cards lately. With the economy down and all the recent tragedies, people aren't buying those edgy, Gen-X cards our designers keep churning out that are the bulk of our line. I've told the design manager this, but his attitude is 'We design the cards, you sell them.' It's killing us." Sam shows the group samples of the best-selling cards from your biggest competitor. They reinforce his analysis. Roses, puppies, and graceful swans are all over them.

You look again at the design manager's business process chart. At no point is any consultation with sales mentioned. You agree with Sam that more consultation should occur. This is no longer some vague personal issue between managers who don't like each other. You have identified an area ripe for a business process improvement.

Implementing an Accountable Process

There are two ways of implementing processes; one is formal, and the other is designed not to scare people who believe that flowcharts are only for sewer systems.

Our bias is naturally the first. We think processes are best designed and communicated visually. All of the flowcharts in this chapter are processes. Start with what you want the outcome to be. Make this the title. Then break down that goal into the steps required to achieve it. Identify the following:

- Expected outcomes
- Number and sequence of steps
- Responsibilities for each step
- Expected time frames for each step
- Deliverables for each step

Draw lines between the steps to identify prerequisites and sequences of events, as in Figure 6–7. Ask your knowledge workers to review, police, improve, and evangelize this.

Blessed simplicity.

However, many people respond much better to an approach called "cheating." After secretly creating your own flowchart, discuss with the program owner the goal you would like to see from the new process. Develop a report that he or she will add to the weekly status report.

For the greeting card improvement initiative, bring in the design manager and the sales manager that you want to have input in the early designs. Explain that we're losing market share, and that's not acceptable. When you ask the design manager for his ideas on changing the situation, explain that we must be more proactive and that your impression, based on looking at the cards that are taking share away from us, is that our sales team is correct.

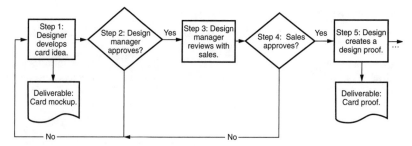

Figure 6–7

So we're going to try a new process here. We're not going to start looking over the designers' shoulders, but we're going to make sure they consider input from the salespeople before they start designing. Prepare a report that looks like Table 6–3. Each one of the columns is designed to tell you something. The card name column identifies the activity being worked on. The design lead and sales lead columns show who is responsible from both groups to sign off on the design. It is important that the report has actual people's names on it, as opposed to generic departments or locations. That way, people have the opportunity to be involved, to be recognized, and to lead a successful program.

The differences between the baseline and the forecast sales approval dates tell you if that step is on track. Implicit in this chart is the idea that sales has to sign off on the idea first. Similarly, the differences between the baseline and the forecast proofs completed dates tell you if that step is on track. Any differences between the baseline and the forecast dates signal that that step is a problem. This report enforces the best practices behavior we wish to see. You want your people to get sales' approval before they get the proofs completed. Every week, when you review this report, you will reinforce this behavior. In this way what you're measuring will get done, and you'll have visibility into how it's going.

Make sure to get this report on a weekly basis. Post it in a public place. Make sure to put it on the intranet. Make sure to send it out to everyone involved. The two leads from design and sales will also quickly realize that everyone in the organization knows that they're responsible and that you will acknowledge their success if they do a good job.

This may or may not solve our problem. You should be open to changing or adding to the process if someone makes a good case for

Table 6-3: Successful Greeting Cards Report

Card Name	Design Lead	Sales Lead	Sales Approval Date		Proofs Completed Date	
			Baseline	Forecast	Baseline	Forecast

why another method may work better. The change in this business process is a starting point, a baseline. If this doesn't work, we may begin a formal new initiative to overhaul our entire creative approach, and we will handle that using the five key phases of project management. We realize that metrics for process improvement in the knowledge arena can be tricky. It may be well and good for the greeting card team to implement this process and get all the boxes filled in in the chart on time, for example, but success will come months down the line only when the cards they produce either sell or do not sell.

Remember that process is not an island, not an end in and of itself. Who cares if you've developed the greatest process in the world if it's not flexible enough to respond to changes in corporate priorities, or if its workers religiously follow its steps despite a changed business climate or financial situation or other variables—in short, if pursuing it does more harm than good? Similarly, you can evaluate your process only if you constantly measure its output through progress tracking (the subject of our next chapter). Only in that way can you continue to improve. And finally, you want the company's knowledge store to be constantly informing and updating and streamlining process. As you work toward transparency, knowledge workers will understand the importance of what they're working on. They will understand the importance of adhering to process and constantly measuring progress against key goals. Ultimately, they should become more open and alert to new ways of delivering value and updating existing processes.

Progress Tracking
Big Brother's Kind but Firm Older Sister

When you cannot measure it, when you cannot express it in numbers, your knowledge is of a meagre and unsatisfactory kind.

—LORD KELVIN[1]

A CARTOON FROM THE 1950s features Ralph Wolf and Sam Sheepdog. Each episode they emerge from their homes, offering a matter of fact "G'morning Ralph" and "G'morning Sam." They walk down the road together and stow their lunch pails by a tree. A factory whistle blows. They punch cards in a time clock, and they spend the episode engaged in all kinds of politically incorrect violence. Ralph, armed with an endless supply of explosives, booby traps, and diversionary tactics, tries to steal the sheep that stalwart Sam guards. Sam always foils Ralph's plan and saves the sheep. Finally, the whistle blows again, their animosity disappears, and they pleasantly stroll home together.

Obviously, this cartoon's humor was aimed at knowledge workers!

One of the things knowledge workers often say they like best about their jobs is that they don't have to punch a time clock. Well, there can be no real understanding and transparency in an organization that does not keep track of the time required to complete key activities and programs. This chapter is about asking for a very specific kind of accountability from your knowledge workers—accountability for their time.

The Status Masterpiece

Our customers despair about the inaccuracy of their forecasts. All too often, knowledge workers indicate that work is coming along very smoothly, often right up until the very last second, when they suddenly appear somber-faced, eyes downcast, with the bad news that Something Has Happened, some unforeseen monkey wrench has clogged the works, and now it will be X more weeks before the activity will be finished. They constantly return to the lament that every activity is so unique, and potential spoilers are so peculiar and unpredictable, they're always in fate's hands.

The problem stems from the way knowledge workers communicate or, more precisely, are allowed to communicate—their activity's status to their management. Managers take their knowledge workers off the hook when it comes to asking for hard numbers and metrics in regard to their work progress. They ask for status reports, but they are willing to entertain enthusiasm reports ("We're doing great!"), or even "status masterpieces" instead—carefully crafted works of art designed to elicit an emotional response like happiness or confidence, regardless of the underlying reality. In these masterpieces, everyone and everything in a team is cast in its most optimistic, enthusiastic light. Meanwhile, external elements such as other teams' contributions are painted at the margins like demons on the borders of ancient maps, threatening the gentle good people of the program within. In these status masterpieces, as much effort is expended planning contingency blame assignment as on genuinely trying to come up with a realistic picture of what's happening.

We're not going to argue that accurate status reports on knowledge work are easy to produce. Remember that earlier example about process? How do you create a status report about the development of an advertising campaign, for example, when the copywriter is still in the sitting-and-looking-out-the-window stage of the activity? If she's spent 2 weeks considering 59 different three-word advertising slogans, is she just getting started, half finished, or minutes from victory? Very hard to say.

Typically an employee's manager writes a status masterpiece that is three parts experience (how long did past activities take her?) and one part enthusiasm report and/or conversational impression ("Um, it's coming along pretty well, I think. Ask me tomorrow") and two parts crossed fingers. The manager isn't trying to mislead his or her managers. The fact is that things can sidetrack a knowledge worker.

Closed-Loop Project Control

HP's Terry Ash, whom we introduced in the last chapter, knows about how progress tracking can inform and enhance closed-loop project control.

"We found that many of our project managers were using fly-by-the-seat-of-the-pants project control techniques," Ash explained. "It is okay to look out the window, see that the weather is fine, and follow your flight plan to your destination. But the weather is often not fine, you encounter turbulence, and you have equipment problems on the plane."

Flying-by-the-seat-of-your-pants project control is evident when one of your people does a lot of work on a new initiative and creates a pretty Gantt chart poster and a project plan using *Microsoft Project*. The stages are neatly spelled out, and hitting the deadline appears not only doable but inevitable. But 6 months later you look at the Gantt chart and ask, "What were we thinking?" Those involved will reply that everything was on track until Something Happened. Something made the assumptions of that chart invalid.

Unfortunately, flying by the seat of his or her pants, the manager did not radio the tower that Something would make an on-time arrival in Cancun unlikely. Instead, the project plane has been circling the Phoenix airport for 3 hours, hopin' and wishin' and prayin' the fog lifts.

Ash's answer to this problem enhances closed-loop project control by providing quantitative real-time progress metrics. It is a system that tracks employees' times and baselines progress constantly off the original plan. Closed-loop project control can handle Something. In fact, it can handle Anything. That's because it's not dependent on an ideal world. It creates a baseline for the schedule and the cost, but it begins reality-checking those estimates right from the get-go, spotting variances and encouraging managers to explore what's either created false assumptions or threatened the integrity of the program and must be dealt with immediately. "Managers now can fly under instrument control and increase the odds of getting there on time and on budget," says Ash.

To implement closed-loop project control, you need to do all the things we've already talked about: You must have a responsive, accountable work culture; and you must align your priorities and implement process. With those elements as a background, the next thing your organization needs to do is track its progress.

The Baseline Plan

As you'll recall from Chapter 6, during the initiation phase of the project management process, an opportunity's expected cost and time frame are noted. During the planning phase, the program's plan is developed, which provides a road map to project completion. This initial plan is very important because it becomes your activity baseline. Progress is always measured off the baseline, which freezes the expected attributes for the program. Those attributes include the following:

- Expected budget, or how much money the program expects to spend in order to achieve the expected results
- Expected time frame, or how much time the program is expected to take in order to achieve the desired results

Using a hypothetical situation to see how progress tracking provides excellent quantitative visibility, let's say your organization is working on a design for a new financial product. Your company's CEO has decreed that it's vital for the company to offer a new derivatives instrument, and she has chosen you to develop it. You ask your team how long it will take to complete the work, and they give you an estimate. Let's say this answer is 10 person months. You run this estimate by the CEO, and she approves it as being realistic. You tell your team to go ahead and begin developing the derivatives instrument. Your team manager tells you that since there are 10 people at his disposal, he should be ready with the new instrument in about a month. This sounds good to you, and you give him the green light.

Why do we need some fancy-sounding thing like closed-loop project control to manage such a simple endeavor? What can go wrong in a month? As a manager about to OK the program plan, you must perform a quick reality check in the three key assumption areas discussed below.

I. Accurate Availability

What other things might your team be working on? When your manager schedules this work, he must estimate his people's availability. This number can be anywhere between zero to 100 percent. In this particular scenario, the manager has assumed that availability for all team members is 100 percent.

Does this number include the work on other programs to which his team members have already committed? Does this number include time off, staff meetings, training, performance reviews, and other equally important activities? There will always be some amount of time spent on necessary tasks not associated with the critical activity.

2. Accurate Start Date

Can all of your manager's people start right away? This assumption can be verified only if your manager knows without a doubt that his people are not working on anything else. How many times have you been told that a particular activity was completed, only to discover weeks later that there are still "just a few loose ends to tie up"? Inaccuracy in setting start dates due to other activities getting pushed out is another major reason that things don't go according to plan.

3. Accurate Work Partitioning

If an activity can be divided easily among many team members with no communication among them and with no interdependencies, then 10 people can complete this task in 1 month. However, knowledge work is more interactive than that, which means that inaccurate work partitioning can quickly make a good plan invalid.

What are the concurrent and serial dimensions to the program plan? Have you aligned the resource availability to reflect that? Have employees scheduled business trips or vacations or other activities during key hand-off stages?

Let's assume that none of these initial incorrect assumptions have occurred and work begins. Now, what must you factor in?

One Crucial Thing: Stuff Happens

This is an entirely new derivatives product; it has never been designed before. It has never been brought to market before. This team has never done anything quite like this before. No matter how similar this derivatives instrument is to any previously designed derivatives instrument, there will be new things and new issues it encounters. Your team, after all, is using its knowledge to create something new. The list of possible curveballs is long: A key player may become ill. Work may be delayed because of a systems crash. There may be a change to securities law that would affect the product, causing development to stall while legal figures out the implications.

Successful people tend to be too optimistic and to ignore the Something that almost always happens. Take Farzad. Every morning, we commute to work together. Every morning, it takes 30 to 35 minutes to travel from our home to the office. If you ask Farzad how long this trip takes, he will tell you, very sincerely, 20 to 25 minutes, and he truly believes this. Why do we differ? Because virtually every single morning Something Happens along the way, such as heavy traffic, an accident, or road work, that extends what should be a 20- to 25-minute trip by 5 to 10 minutes. So you can reliably insert that 5- to 10-minute delay into the process of our commute. Any calculation you make based on the timing (how early we should leave, how much longer it will take to arrive) likely will be encumbered by a delay of that length. However, Farzad clings to the perfect scenario of no traffic and no delays as the benchmark and "normal" condition because he likes to assume the best. If he overhears me tell someone the trip takes 35 minutes, he will interject, "Oh, that was just because of traffic. Normally it takes 20 to 25 minutes."

You can't typically prevent at least some Stuff from happening. But the important thing is: Do your people update their managers? Do you know the real-time status of your people's progress? As the work progresses, are your people's estimates available and accurate?

Our new aim, now that we've put those status masterpieces behind us, is to bravely deal with these new realities. To do that, you must constantly monitor and improve the accuracy of your plan. If conditions change, you should know instantly so you can react. Straight out of the gate, you need to check your plan. You need to constantly recheck it going forward.

Progress tracking is this constant verification. Progress tracking is the periodic reporting of two metrics:

- The actual amount of time expended on an activity
- The estimated amount of time it will require to complete the activity

That's the estimate to complete, or ETC. Progress tracking is typically considered on a weekly basis. Workers report the amount of time they spend on their activities. They submit these reports to their managers, who approve or reject them. This information is then used to update the schedule. Here is a sample of an employee's basic time sheet:

Employee	Hours Worked on Derivatives Program	ETC
John	45	50

This particular time sheet shows that John is spending 100 percent of his time on the derivatives program because that is the only activity listed. This is what you need, it is what you asked for, and it is what you are getting. You are reassured. What if the time sheet above showed 30 hours on the derivatives program, 10 hours on some other program, and a 65-hour ETC? And what if John reported that he spent the other 10 hours last week cleaning up loose ends on another activity? Well, you would probably have a conversation with John to find out why he was still working on a low-priority task when the derivatives program was mission critical. Depending on John's explanation, you would either tell him to continue to use his judgment about which program to spend his time on, or you would tell him he is not to go near anything but the derivatives program until further notice. In either event, you would have spotted a potential problem early and investigated it.

As the rest of your reports file their time sheets, you begin to see who is the busiest and how you might better balance the workload; you get a timely alert to emerging problems; you get a range of ETCs that may align or be highly contradictory—again exposing a problem you need to solve quickly. You have improved your visibility dramatically. It is important to keep in mind that a team member is much more comfortable reporting a realistic even if unfavorable ETC than a realistic but unfavorable end date. In other words, a team member would rather say to you, "The program will take 2 weeks of work to complete (even though the target end date is 1 week from now)" than say, "You know what? We're going to be 1 week late."

Finally, according to many of our customers, you stand a good chance of improving employees' morale by providing them with an environment that promotes efficiency and timely management attention. Since progress tracking gives you, as their manager, an unbiased view of what they are working on and how hard they are working on it, many of your knowledge workers will come to feel that their work is more appreciated.

This is true because of the proverbial Hawthorne effect. For those who are unfamiliar with this, the *Hawthorne effect* refers to an improvement in a work process caused by active management observation of that process. It comes from a series of studies conducted at Western Electric's Hawthorne plant outside of Chicago. These studies were conducted from 1927 to 1932 by Harvard Business School professor Elton Mayo.[2] He was trying to understand the effect of work conditions on workers' productivity. Professor Mayo studied how varying rest breaks and hours and environmental factors like heat, humidity, and light levels affected factory workers' productivity. To conduct the study, he took a small team of workers away from the assembly line. He changed their supervisor and their working conditions, always discussing these changes in advance. He measured their productivity before and after making the changes. The supervisor stayed with the workers— talking with them, updating them on the experiment, listening to their advice and complaints.

The results confused Professor Mayo: Output kept going up. Mayo decreased working hours, and output went up. He increased working hours, and output went up. He gave them more breaks, and output went up. He gave them fewer breaks, and output went up. He gave them free meals, and output went up.

Professor Mayo concluded that the workers had formed a social group and that the social group was doing the motivating. They liked the increased management attention and the feeling of specialness that participation in the study entailed. By being picked to participate in the study, the workers felt proud. Their positive relationship with the supervisor and the fact that he discussed changes in advance with them made them want to succeed. Even when negative changes occurred, like taking away rest breaks, the workers accepted it because they had been consulted beforehand.

The simple fact is, if you pay attention to something as a manager, it is more likely to get done than something you don't pay attention to. This goes back to Farzad's comment that the best way to reward knowledge workers is to give them your time and attention. How did people forget that? When did they fall into the trap of thinking that all these artists had to be left alone in order to do their best work?

Improvements to Look for from Progress Tracking

Our customers have identified six benefits of instituting progress tracking, and they say the benefits come virtually immediately.

I. Improved Estimates

Now you've got data. Constantly confronting unrealistic estimates tends to push people toward making more realistic estimates.

2. Identification of Problems in Real Time

Perhaps you can step in and change course, add new resources, or otherwise minimize whatever problem is slowing up the work.

3. Measurable Efficiencies

With data, you can monitor which teams are producing more with less time expended. That allows you to contrast the efforts and styles and processes and standardize on the most efficient.

4. Improved Visibility to Critical Activities

A wonderful thing happens when you start to track time: Unimportant activities get exposed, and important activities get the right attention.

It's an interesting quirk of human nature that some people are drawn to low-priority work because it seems doable versus high-priority work that may carry an element of uncertainty that creates fear of failure.

5. Measurable Actual Availability

A senior VP commits a drive-by and wants three of your people for a "quick" pet project. With an accurate picture of your team's current availability and utilization, you can have a very different kind of conversation than you could if a senior executive simply asked: "How busy are your people these days?" and piled on another assignment. When you have tracking data in hand, you can paint a picture of how a new assignment will threaten the ETC of a key initiative and make sure that the senior executive is aware of the quantitative impact of his or her request.

6. Reducing Recurring Errors and Rework

Here at Niku, our senior vice president and chief technology officer, Mark Moore, has implemented progress tracking in his organization, and he has created a specific category called *do-over tasks*. This do-over time was time that people said they devoted to doing work that they had previously thought had been completed, either because of mistakes, inefficiencies, or bad decisions. This rework percentage is currently at 5 percent. Arriving at this figure is a creative use of progress tracking to capture a snapshot of a problem that is cutting across teams and even departments. Once identified as a time drain, the reasons for the rework can now be explored and acted on.

All Good Things

Progress tracking requires a certain amount of management sensitivity and finesse. The issue comes down to one of control: How much perceived control can management exert in a knowledge worker organization without the workers' rebelling? There is one story about implementing progress tracking that resulted in 10 percent of the organization just getting up and walking out.

Let's address this realistically. First, managers need to understand the landmines associated with progress tracking.

As you get ready to roll this out, be prepared for negative feedback. Knowledge workers' objections will fall into two categories: First, they will flash on all the things they do during the day that have nothing to do with work—phone calls to their spouses, updating their online fantasy baseball team scores, gossiping by the water cooler. Some will become paranoid and convince themselves you're just gathering evidence to can them. They will make cracks about Big Brother.

Confront this head on. Without using a "gotcha" tone, explain to them right off the bat you are not implementing this process in order to "get" anyone. You are implementing it to get data on the organization so that you can substantiate its value and improve its productivity. As we said earlier in the book, mature, professional employees must realize that the company owns their working hours, their equipment, even their Internet connection. (Frankly, one does not need progress tracking in order to identify employees who are spending inordinate amounts of time online at inappropriate Web sites or chat rooms. The IT department can produce a nice little report on that in two shakes.)

The second type of push-back you'll likely get is that every knowledge worker's job situation is exceptional and doesn't lend itself to time-tracking. These employees will not want to be pinned down by estimates, or baselines, or periodic reporting. You are going to hear a lot of whining about how it's impossible to quantify the creative process or summon brilliance for precisely 8 hours per day.

Nod your head, bite your lip, make sympathetic noises, and let them know you realize that each person making this lament is unique—just like everyone else. But do not let them off the hook. You are not here to shelter and feed tenured philosophers grappling with the meaning of life. This is a commercial enterprise, and you are paying them to work, to deliver value in a timely way, and to coordinate their efforts with other employees trying to do the same thing. Be sympathetic. But explain to them that tracking progress is not an individual performance evaluation. This process is designed to track the progress of clearly identified, highly important activities for the good of the organization.

Another source of concern is overzealous managers. The mere thought of so much good information sometimes sways people's judgment, and they start looking for witches to burn. Their little shoulder devil starts telling them, "I can finally prove that Randolph takes way too many trips to Starbucks."

This is a good time to recall the Hawthorne effect again: Another part of the Hawthorne studies was not so positive. In this case, studying a different group of workers who distrusted the supervisor had entirely different results. These employees thought that the supervisor was out to trick them into increasing their production without an increase in pay. Their productivity actually declined no matter what the supervisors did.

If you try to implement progress tracking with the wrong motivation, you will get the wrong results. Make sure progress tracking is implemented simply to track progress on important initiatives and that your managers are warned they should not even joke about it being used to expose slackers. Honestly, there is so much good, useful information that helps productivity, and so much to act on, that the negative information simply gets buried. Fixing Randolph's Starbucks habit is best left to direct discussion, not a sneaky little progress tracking report.

Having told them all of the above, your little secret is that you *are* going to use this process to show your boss and your customers just how wonderful and hardworking your people are, and how important to the organization your team is. We find that lots of internal service providers have trouble justifying their existences inside large companies, especially when a slower economy has put the spotlight on cutting costs. Make sure your people know that you know how hard they are working. Acknowledge to those above you that your people are working on the things that matter. Broadcast that they are working hard. This will create your own personal enhanced Hawthorne effect.

Knowledge workers are motivated to work on challenging things, interesting programs, cutting-edge stuff. They do this because they want to exercise their minds, they want to learn and use their knowledge, because they want to be important. When faced with obvious management ignorance, they lose interest rapidly. Not understanding how hard your people are working, or allowing them to wander off on programs they don't realize are low priority, is a toxic form of management ignorance.

Painless Progress Tracking

I offer you here some tactical steps that companies have used in implementing progress tracking.

The Most Important Thing

Our customers agree: The single most important thing in implementing progress tracking is active management involvement. If management never looks at the data about how hard their people are working, their people will quickly realize that progress tracking is not important. Compliance and management involvement are highly correlated. You and your managers should review results weekly and post the results where all employees see them. An e-mail to those who are slacking off about reporting their time and progress each week will keep compliance in line.

Once you get your employees in the habit of reporting their two key metrics—effort expended and ETC—you need to compile that data into two kinds of reports for your organization. The process goes like this: Once the manager approves, the information is gathered in one place and used to update schedules with new ETC information. This is what gives you closed-loop project control. As knowledge workers react to issues, new information, setbacks, and other stuff, they update the system with the new ETCs. This information is then used to update the schedule.

Figure 7–1 shows how a schedule is updated with information from progress tracking. Before updating, the plan shows that the "design pricing" task is expected to take 50 hours. This figure is from the baseline plan that was frozen during the planning phase of the project management process. A knowledge worker then enters her time and notes that she spent 40 hours last week on the pricing design. She also notes that she thinks it's going to take another 20 hours to complete this task.

This gives you a very important piece of information. This tells you that, instead of taking 50 hours, as expected, this task will take 60 hours (the 40 already expended plus the 20 ETC). If another task is dependant on the design pricing task being complete, then that task is going to slip.

Real-World Progress Tracking

Richard Whelchel, of Coca-Cola Bottling Consolidated, has successfully implemented progress tracking in his organization. In Chapter 4 we discussed Whelchel's impact on his organization. Time tracking was one of his biggest challenges:

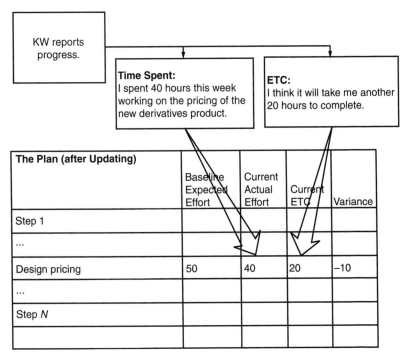

Figure 7–1

I was looking at an organization whose culture could not understand time entry. . . . There was a cultural change associated with getting people to account for their time. The key to it being, once you start to measure me, what happens to my job? Do you find out that you don't need me?

But we overcame that by posing this question: How many people in this room have been involved in projects for which you have worked your steady 40 hours a week thinking everything's hunky dory, and then 3 weeks before delivery you start working evenings and weekends, 7 days a week, to try to get to something that you can deliver? And then, do you deliver less than you promised and at lower quality than you promised? And every hand went up! That was my in to say: Give me a shot at this time entry thing, and I will try to use it to make your lives manageable. Over the next couple of projects, we were able to work 40 to 45 hours a week right up to cutover week (a switch to a new system—ordinarily the type of event that requires marathon hours), and then we worked the cutover conversion over the weekend and went live on Monday morning. That was a bit of a coup for us.

Whelchel demonstrates how much visibility can be achieved through progress tracking. His organization can report to the CEO, telling him that the organization is on schedule and on budget. What would Chuck have given for that?

The Mechanics

Here is how a weekly reporting cycle works. Everyone tracks his or her progress weekly. This includes both time spent as well as the ETC. This progress needs to be reported to the manager no later than 10:00 A.M. Monday morning. Managers then need to review these over the next couple of hours. Progress is posted to a central location, whether it's a wall, or a whiteboard, or a database, or a Web page. This should be completed by noon on Monday. This then gives everyone Monday afternoon to synchronize the data from progress tracking and update all the plan information. New information is incorporated into everyone's plans. This may result in schedules shifting, which may increase effort or cost variances, which would then trigger the correcting phase for the project management process. That's a weekly reporting cycle. The department head is updated every week, using status reports. Everything is consolidated on a monthly basis to the CEO.

Using the Information: Closed-Loop Project Control

Progress tracking is an easy-to-understand mechanism for reporting on schedule and cost performance. If you have followed the system, then you established a baseline for all your programs back in the planning phase of the project management process. With progress tracking, you constantly refer back to this baseline, using the most up-to-date information, to see your variances. You should review these to spot trouble programs. They are easy to spot; they are the ones with a really big variance.

An example of a *variance report* is in Figure 7–2. You can tell which programs are the trouble programs by looking at the variance percentage columns. There are four columns for schedule and four columns for cost information. The baseline columns come from the baseline information from the planning phase of the project management process. The forecast information is the amount to date, plus the ETCs. The baseline end date and the forecast end date are expressed in person days of effort, for easier variance computation. The variance column is the difference between the baseline and the forecast. Negative variances are bad; positive variances are good. The variance percent is the variance divided by the baseline.

The "on-time-and-budget" program is fine: Its effort variance is 2 percent unfavorable, and its cost variance is 4 percent favorable. The "late-and-over-budget" program, on the other hand, is a disaster, with effort and cost variances of 34 and 24 percent, both unfavorable. This is a trouble program. If you use a baseline and progress tracking, you can quickly see which programs are trouble programs and act on them quickly.

You can do a lot with this information. For example, to really understand your bottlenecks, you can take a look at the variances on a step-by-step basis. You can do this for all programs that follow a particular business

Program	Schedule, Effort in Person Days				Cost, in $000s			
	Baseline	Forecast	Variance	Variance Percent	Baseline	Forecast	Variance	Variance Percent
On time and budget	100	102	-2	-2	50	47.8	2.2	4
Late and over budget	100	134	-34	-34	50	62	-12	-24
Total	200	236	-36	-18	100	109.8	-9.8	-10

Figure 7–2

Risk Analysis Programs*	Planned Effort	Actual Effort	Variance	Variance Percent
Feasibility Studies				
Meet with client and /or business unit.	47	49	-2	-4%
Conduct interview.	107	129	-22	-21%
Analyze information.	23	21.7	1.3	6%
Prepare draft.	56	50	6	11%
Present draft to management.	35	34.5	0.5	1%
Refine draft.	56	58.9	-2.9	-5%
Make final presentation.	34	32.3	1.7	5%
Total	358	375.4	-17.4	-5%

* Data from 10 programs

Figure 7–3

process. For example, you can do some analysis regarding the last 10 times your organization created a feasibility study. Take a look at Figure 7–3. You can see that step 2, the interview step, is the problem child. A similar analysis can show you where the problems are within your organization, within your best practices, and help you fix them to improve your entire organization's productivity. Note that all programs, in total, do not yield a horrible variance percent—it's only 5 percent. With progress tracking, you can get some pretty detailed information about your organization's productivity.

Also, you could show your on-time and on-budget percentages in a chart that resembles Figure 7–4. Here is a handy way to show your manager just how brilliant you and your organization really are. You can see that the organization delivers programs with less than a 10 percent cost overrun 98 percent of the time.

Another good report is an *alignment report*, an example of which is shown in Figure 7–5. If you've categorized your portfolio, you can use the information you get from progress tracking to verify alignment. You can compare your actual efforts with the efforts you are supposed to be allocating to the different categories in your portfolio. You can roll up your progress information by category and verify that your actual allocations match your targets for strategic initiatives and management objectives. The report shown in the figure reveals that the organization is spending too much time on new product development and not enough time on customer satisfaction.

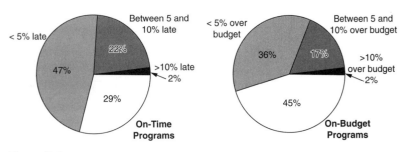

Figure 7–4

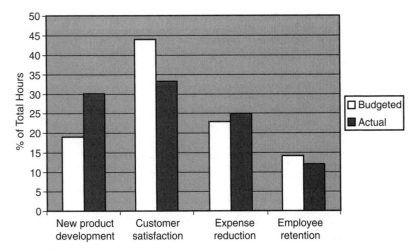

Figure 7–5

Pitfalls

When we talk about progress tracking, we get a lot of nodding of heads, particularly at director levels and above. They say, "That's a great idea, those people over there should use it." Progress tracking, like cutting down on coffee, is something best done by somebody else. The fact is, however, progress tracking is good for everyone. To get a system up and running and keep it running well in your organization, try to avoid the following pitfalls.

I. Needless Detail

Many organizations feel that they can't get any benefit from progress tracking unless they track down to the minute. If you have the urge to track down to the minute, our advice is: Sit down before you hurt your-self. The administrative overhead associated with this level of progress tracking typically overshadows any benefits the organization can get from it.

Another detail-related problem arises if, after failing to derail Randolph, the little shoulder devil regroups and starts mounting a campaign against bureaucracy. That horrible HR director's process for annual reviews takes up way too much time, doesn't it? Isn't the director always calling meetings to talk about annual reviews? The importance of annual reviews, the forms to fill out for annual reviews, the way to conduct annual reviews, and on and on and on. Aren't they a terrific waste of time? Somebody comes to you: Let's track the amount of effort that goes into THAT! Let's make sure that the admin bucket is broken down into all the tasks that the evil HR director wants to accomplish.

Do not be sucked into this abyss of needless detail. Concentrate on tracking what matters. Progress tracking is to be used for important initiatives and activities inside the company that are critical to its success. If your HR director is truly impacting productivity at a meaningful level, the "admin" column of everyone's time sheets will be stratospheric whether or not you add to their burden by breaking down all the little components.

2. 40-Hour Hard Stop

In the beginning weeks of implementing a progress tracking system, people are usually hesitant to enter anything greater than 40 hours for a week or 4 weeks for a month. They usually believe that this is what their managers want to see. In reality, the integrity of the time data is at risk. The data are at risk because that's not what people really did. If your people are hiding the work they do, you will not be able to understand what it truly takes to deliver your work. If it really takes 50 hours a week but your people report only 40 hours, you will continue to schedule them to deliver 50 hours of work every week since that's what you think it takes.

You may think it takes 1 week to do the design for that new derivatives instrument, but it really takes 58 hours, and people are working 58 hours to deliver it. You will never know that you are overworking your people. You will think everything is just fine, but your guys are being habitually overworked. From the start, demand real data. Why does it take so long? If it really takes that long, let's schedule it that way. People will start to praise you and start saying things like, "No one has ever understood us before."

To fix this problem, you must understand your people's work habits. Are they there at 7:00 in the evening? If they are, and they turn in 40 hours per week, question them on it. They will be impressed that you noticed, and they will be impressed that you care.

3. The Brian Effect

We've named this problem after a worker who was exceptional in every way but one. Brian worked 28 hours a day and would do anything for the company, except turn in his time. It was really difficult for his manager to bug him about this because he was just so darn good at everything else he was supposed to do. Not tracking his progress seemed so trivial a fault that his manager was embarrassed to bring it up.

Other people, believing (sometimes erroneously) that they were just as important to the organization as Brian, started questioning why they had to do it and he didn't. And then, they decided that it was a task that really didn't need to be done by them either. Of course, compliance started to creep down.

We solved this problem by creating a progress tracking Wall of Shame. On it, at the end of the day on Monday, we posted the names of all those who didn't turn in their time cards. Including the managers, and including Brian. Now, I can't say that Brian always turns in his time card. But he does it a lot more often than he did before, and nobody else is questioning whether Brian gets special treatment.

4. Just Going through the Motions

Two managers from Accenture in the Metro Center, Licia Knight and Nancy Simonson, raise another important issue involving progress tracking. When they first implemented a progress tracking system for a big program, they still weren't getting solid schedule end dates. Things would be going fine, right up until the last week, and then schedules would slip by a few weeks or worse. They knew that progress tracking should be able to stop this problem, so they took a close look at the numbers. People's ETCs were both wrong and widely variable. This meant that people were not really progress tracking; they were only going through the motions. They were still trying to create status masterpieces.

In Figure 7–6, in the "going-through-the-motions" scenario, you can see that the variability in estimates to complete varied wildly. This is because people were not paying attention. They were not really thinking about what it was going to take to complete this activity. Simonson and Knight saw this type of behavior and recognized it right away.

The real issue was that people were managing the day-to-day using spreadsheets, bar napkins, any handy piece of paper. They reported their progress from these pieces of paper. They were then "going through the motions" to meet the minimum information management needs of their superiors. Simonson and Knight wanted them, rather, to manage day-to-day with real data derived from progress tracking.

To fix it, they started reporting on the variability in ETCs. They plotted how closely the actual ETCs matched the planned ETCs week by week. They were then able to identify the managers who were just going through the motions. With a little help from management, these managers were able to see how beneficial it would be to pay attention to establishing accurate ETCs.

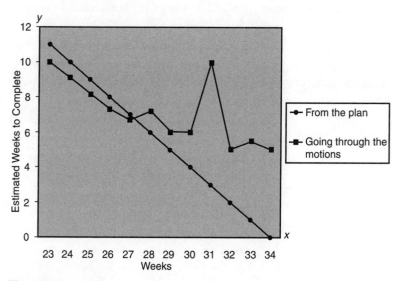

Figure 7–6

When the system was being used correctly by their organization, Knight and Simonson were able to solve their center's biggest problem. Both work for Steve Saba, the center director, who once told us, "All I want is to get the demand side to see how the supply side is being used." One of his big problems was to be able to show that his resources were being allocated and tracked for optimal product delivery. Simply stated, he needed to ensure that an hour burned was an hour earned.

For Saba, progress tracking = happy customers.

The Cost

It takes a little effort to track your progress. It typically takes a worker 15 minutes per week to report on his or her project status. It typically takes 15 minutes per week per manager to manage this activity.

We must stress that there's no reason to track progress if there is no executive oversight. People will not track their time if no one is watching. It is therefore important to develop a system that can automate these tasks and provide meaningful executive-level reports. These will enable upper management to fix all the problems that the reports highlight. In return, the company will see improved efficiency, better estimates, real-time problem identification, quantitative metrics on progress, and improved visibility.

In the beginning weeks of implementing a progress tracking system, don't be discouraged if only 50 percent of your people do it. It typically takes a month or two to get everyone in the swing of things. But, if you look at the progress reports on a weekly basis and pay attention to the missing progress reports, you can get the data to where it's 95 or 97 percent accurate. That's pretty much as good as it's going to get.

Once you have progress tracking in place, start looking at your variance reports. This can give you a quick guide as to the elements of your programs where trouble is likely to flare up. Contrary to past experience, you'll come to realize spontaneous combustion is quite rare.

CHAPTER

8

Working Smarter

Unleashing the Genius of Your Organization through Knowledge Management

U NDERSTANDING WHAT YOUR PEOPLE KNOW and putting that capital to use every day for the good of the organization are the crux of a vexing proposition in the knowledge workplace. Knowledge is expensive to develop—yet it evaporates when unattended. Plus, some workers hoard knowledge. Others never connect with the people who could benefit from their knowledge in time to help.

A former Oracle colleague named Bill was trying to sign up a new software reseller in Brazil several years ago. He was having a very hard time with this reseller because Oracle needed a Brazilian government agency to okay the deal. This frustrating, chaotic government agency's representatives wouldn't return calls, and agreements that were made one day were revised the next.

In the middle of this, Bill's assistant went on maternity leave and he got a temporary assistant, assigned randomly from the human resources pool. This temporary assistant learned what Bill was trying to do and asked him one day, "Do you know my background?" Bill didn't. She explained that she had been the assistant to an undersecretary of state for Latin American affairs in Jimmy Carter's administration. Her job was to work with Latin American dignitaries and keep track of everyone's preferences for food, alcohol, accommodations, and so on. She still had many contacts in Brazil, and she introduced Bill to them.

Bill was able to get the agreement with the reseller completed within a few weeks—the Brazilian equivalent of light speed.

The assistant's contribution was fantastically serendipitous. Bill would no more have thought to ask the HR pool for an assistant with contacts in the Brazilian commerce department than he would have asked for an assistant who could trim a mainsail on a schooner. Yet, leveraging her knowledge provided enormous value to the organization.

As organizations grow, their knowledge capital grows exponentially as they add people and they add their people's experiences. But you look at Bill's Brazilian deal and understandably think: "It's impossible to come up with a system that could have predicted or created this scenario."

It was lucky. But we believe that technology has developed to a point where a savvy organization can capture all kinds of valuable knowledge, much of it currently hidden, and use it to help everyone work smarter. Even more important, systems can now organize and integrate far more routine and repeated work processes and work products from knowledge workers, and make them accessible throughout an organization so that the wheel isn't reinvented day after day. In this chapter, we're going to discuss ways to better capture and share knowledge using these new systems. In addition, we will consider knowledge as being either explicit or tacit.

If only it were as simple a matter as buying a shrink-wrapped software program called "Useful and Even Serendipitous Knowledge 2.0" and loading it up. Instead, better knowledge management requires the kind of cultural environment we've advocated in this book, and the rigorous management processes and tools we've described that have been the bedrock of successful business for decades. With those in place, we believe companies now have access to technology that offers dramatic potential to leverage knowledge capital as never before. For purposes of full disclosure, it happens that our company makes that kind of software. In fact, the path we took to understanding the most common knowledge workplace problems is what reinforced for us the management principles we have described in this book. Without good management, technology solutions simply drain resources. They are only as good as the people who deploy them.

A Little History

Say "knowledge management" to many folks in software or big corporate IT departments, and watch lips curl. The first generation of knowledge management software solutions, to put it politely, were time-consuming, clumsy flops. Beginning around the early 1980s, stand-alone knowledge management systems were touted as the first sort of wide-scale artificial intelligence. Like much first-generation software, they were discrete systems that did not synchronize with or even connect to any other systems in the company. They were essentially just large databases of facts and documents that could be searched.

Developers of these systems did a lot of work creating elaborate knowledge taxonomies to hold this knowledge and creating incentives (like $5 for each document added to the knowledge management system) for people to share their knowledge. They had to create those incentives because these early systems demanded that people specifically and deliberately input knowledge. Employees literally did their work, then created a report about the "knowledge" they had collected or generated in the course of doing that. Each person had to make decisions about what classifications he or she would use to describe and file this data for later retrieval.

For example, imagine that you were a consultant to an Alaskan pipeline project for 2 months. You would go to the knowledge database when it was all over and start typing a report. Early on when you were full of energy you might add all kinds of great details—perhaps an evaluation of local engineers capable of inspecting and repairing oil-drilling equipment (should that be tagged "local service providers" or "equipment"?), and another memo on the implications of pending legislation addressing transporting oil in the state of Alaska. Your brain might be on fire with all kinds of other knowledge you picked up, but it doesn't take long before you are trying to end this onerous chore as quickly as possible. And so a lot of knowledge evaporates.

In general, these repository-style systems failed because they did not address the way people actually worked in that they created separate processes designed to hold and manage knowledge that were apart from standard work processes. They required a knowledge worker to separate his or her daily activities into those generating knowledge that must be input, and a vast, amorphous bucket of miscellaneous knowledge and experience that might actually be quite useful to the organization but which the worker had an incentive not to mention since it required more work to enter it into the system.

When Rhonda worked at Arthur Young, now Ernst & Young, she used one of these early systems. As she worked on engagements, completed work products—reports, in other words—went directly to a knowledge repository group. This group scrubbed them of proprietary information, categorized them, and stored them in the repository. Unfortunately, sometimes the work products were scrubbed so much that they had no value. Also, the taxonomies were a killer! In order to attempt to define exactly the type of knowledge they were holding, the systems relied on an elaborately tiered filing language that would describe in excruciating detail just what type of knowledge they were holding. It wasn't enough to say that a document was a quality plan for visual inspection of assemblies on a manufacturing floor and file it under "Quality plans." You had to file it under:

Industry classification: Manufacturing
Industry subclassification: Discrete manufacturing
Industry sub-subclassification: Electronic components
Business process: Finished-goods assembly
Business subprocess: Visual inspection
Document type: Plan
Document subtype: Quality plan

Not only was all this information onerous to enter, if a document was misfiled under an incorrect or vague classification, it might never be seen again.

Knowledge often loses its meaning if it is taken out of context. Tom Berquist, a managing director at Goldman Sachs, told me about his experience with a knowledge management system. The financial analysts began storing all their sales presentations in a knowledge repository. Each presentation followed a similar format: setup, data, conclusions, recommendations, and next steps. They decided to keep intact all presentations in the repository. That way, all analysts would have access to the full context and could mine this storehouse of knowledge for reusable material.

What happened was that analysts couldn't apply the specific case studies to the situations at hand particularly well because so often the facts of their own cases were just different enough to reduce the value of the example. Instead, the analysts came to use this system in an interesting way that actually ignored about 90 percent of the data in the presentations: They simply used the repository to find out who in the firm understood a particular kind of situation. They then picked up the phone to contact the expert, or sent an e-mail. In this case, the system became less a collection of knowledge assets and more a giant, intelligent phone directory.

First-generation approaches to knowledge management were based on discrete chunks of information that could be copied, modified, rearranged, and repurposed for different clients. But interchangeable chunks don't end up being all that useful for most knowledge organizations. Context is crucial to effective knowledge management, and experience yields a plethora of one-of-a-kind knowledge bullets that are hard to categorize and retrieve efficiently.

Aiming for More Intelligent Knowledge Management

The journey to improving your company's knowledge intelligence begins in our two favorite places: culture and disciplined portfolio management. If an organization launches, manages, and tracks programs on a haphazard basis, putting its faith in smart "get its" who disappear for weeks at a time, occasionally throwing a wadded-up progress report over the transom saying that things are "fine," it is simply herding knowledgeable cats. You'll be lucky to make any progress at all.

Even among fairly accountable companies, however, we see tremendous opportunity for improvement in the way they capture and redeploy their knowledge capital. In so many of these companies, knowledge workers' early learning endeavors are like the starship *Enterprise*'s ongoing mission—to seek knowledge by bounding from planet to planet, hoping to find breathable air and nourishment, getting into high-adrenaline confrontations, feeling alternately overconfident and doomed. Along the way, the best ones always develop a profound sense of frustration, which, if the organization acted a little more rationally and used its intellectual capital better, its productivity would be much improved.

That said, there are hopeful signs out there. For example, most organizations have embraced e-mail to facilitate communication and collaboration, and that has provided a big boost to helping people work together more efficiently and to share lots of different kinds of information. E-mail does a large number of things very well, particularly for members of the same team. Because it is easily stored and searched by such variables as date, sender, recipients, and subject, and its contents can be searched by keywords, it is a wonderful tool for a given team or a given project.

As seen through the prism of the entire organization, however, the value of e-mail is more limited. It is not particularly useful for interteam or interinitiative communication. It is difficult to transfer knowledge from one initiative to the next, since there is no historical record or traceability other than the one an individual painstakingly re-creates based on his or her own memory of stored knowledge from previous projects. If you're at home, sick, and your coworker is working on an Alaskan pipeline project, for example, she can't search your e-mail archives to find your historical knowledge. These personal productivity tools help us become individually more productive, but they do not really help the organization become more productive.

The collaboration tools presently on the market represent a step in the right direction. Examples of these would be *Lotus Notes* or *WebEx*. These systems try to get people to work more effectively together by bringing them together to participate in active dialogues for a common cause. They may allow real-time conferencing in which documents can be shared over a network, for example, or they may allow check-in and check-out of documents for use by any member of a team that is allowed access to the program. They allow threaded discussions so many people can ring in with ideas and suggestions and sign off on documents.

But most collaboration systems have the same faults as the other early, stand-alone knowledge management systems—namely, they are separate from the real business process, and they are seen as a sort of extra step that is performed either in parallel with actual work or after real work is done.

When Rhonda was a consultant at Arthur Young, her manager wanted consultants to list the skills each had in a skills bank. Management was then going to use the information for more effective staffing on future initiatives. However, they were busy people. Remembering to update skills the instant a consultant gained new experience was low on the priority list. Therefore, it was no surprise that many of the skills in the skills repository did not accurately represent what people knew how to do because it was always notoriously out of date (see Figure 8–1).

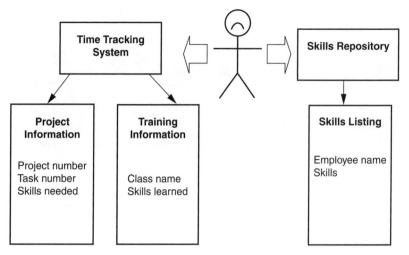

Figure 8–1

Notice, however, the left side of the chart. Notice that on the "time tracking system" side of the equation, information about our skills was, in fact, captured. If we took specific training classes, for example, that information was captured by the time tracking system. Or if we participated in projects that demanded specific skills, that information was also noted. Plus, the domains in which we were working were captured in the project information database—nuclear power, manufacturing, oil industry consulting, greeting card development, whatever. What's more, somewhere in the human resource department, our résumés were on file, listing our education, past jobs, languages we spoke, and the two years we spent living in South America. Extending this line of thinking even more, what about the e-mail Rhonda sent to a colleague when he asked if a class was worthwhile—a six-paragraph summary of what she got out of the experience and more detail on how it applied to the colleague's engagements.

As you can see, the institution already "knew" about Rhonda's baseline skills (her résumé), the training she received to update her skills, and the on-the-job experience she'd amassed. It may even have possessed a few silicon tidbits in its e-mail server that might have been useful if the firm needed a Spanish speaker who knew something about teaching project management skills to oil-drilling engineers. But the system wasn't thinking straight. It didn't know it knew these things because the systems in which those facts resided didn't talk to each other very well. So the system wanted Rhonda to perform a redundant act and list them separately. Silly system.

The Right Way

Knowledge management systems deserved the bad rap they received because they couldn't truly capture information in the context of how people worked. The good news is, new systems like ours can do just that. Let's start with how it can handle explicit knowledge, and then discuss how it can enhance the sharing of tacit knowledge.

Explicit Knowledge

From the early days of intranets, companies have been placing huge amounts of information in databases that employees can access with a browser. This has been an excellent way to store and hold data where it can be easily searched and accessed—vendor lists, huge genomic sequence databases for biotech companies, detailed specs for hardware products, details about the company's 401(k) or its health plan. And then there are all kinds of external, subject-specific databases a company's employees might want to use, and to which the company allows access. All those are perfectly fine uses of data repositories.

Reference data should not be confused with knowledge, however. Data alone does not equal knowledge or wisdom. Specifically, information on how *we* do things, want to do things, should do things, and have done things is much harder to capture. Effective sales presentations, or lists of employee skills, or the process charts for developing new greeting cards, don't do well in repositories. They get neglected. They lose currency. They lose context. And their info can be difficult to retrieve.

Let us try to explain the value of a more accessible system by considering a very difficult type of knowledge management problem: Let's say you run a graphic design consulting firm with about 20 partners, and you've noticed a wide divergence in their ability to generate and manage their projects—typically presentation services for clients who need audio and/or visual support for kicking off major advertising campaigns. Four partners are home-run hitters; at least half a dozen do a decent job; the bottom 10 are very talented designers, but they are lousy salespeople, and they'll be late to their own funerals.

So let's say the basic deliverables from the designers in the management of this project are the following:

- The sales presentation
- The contract spelling out the details of the work
- The presentation services to be delivered to client
- The invoice to the client

Meanwhile you're thinking you'd like to find a way to reuse the knowledge of your best partners. First, you set up a bare-bones system based on a repository approach. You create four databases in which documents can live, and then you ask your four sluggers to give you their "stuff," and you tell the others to go in there and learn learn learn.

Six months from now, you check on how things are going and you discover the pattern is the same: The four sluggers keep slugging, the middle zone continues apace, the lower tier isn't making much progress. You talk to your customers, and you ask a few who've been pitched by both a slugger and a laggard, what made the difference. And they reply that the sluggers all added value. For example, during the sales presentation, the sluggers provided some market analysis data about competitive products, and, before billing, the sluggers each sent a separate risk analysis report, with suggestions for confronting various scenarios. This risk analysis had been a big help to several clients and prompted them to return to the firm again and again.

So now you drive back to the office grinding your molars. The big guns held out on you a little bit. Clearly they had developed a little extra secret sauce that was keeping them ahead of the pack. You get to the office and look at the knowledge repository you'd set up. Uh-oh. It looks like Figure 8–2.

You then realize that you had doomed that knowledge to disappear because of the buckets you set up. "Knowledge management is a crock," you hiss. "What knowledge workers do is impossible to quantify or control."

Not so fast. The problem here is the impossibility of coming up with taxonomies that apply to the myriad variations knowledge workers confront. The repository had a home for the general deliverables all the partners used. But because it didn't have a home for the two extra ones that a few outstanding employees had come to use, that knowledge was

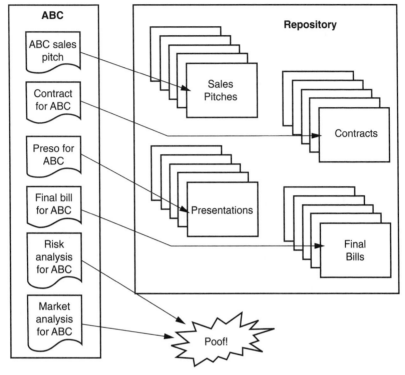

Figure 8–2

lost. Now remember, we're still talking about explicit knowledge, stuff you can write down. A market analysis and a risk analysis are specific things. They were developed on company computers, printed on company printers, exchanged via company e-mail, all on company time in pursuit of business designed to make the enterprise a success. You own that knowledge, and employees have no right to hoard it. Now, how can you capture it? How can you make sharing knowledge as natural as hitting "send" on an e-mail program?

You must use an enterprise-wide solution. Ours is called *Niku 6*. Like this book, it is based on the input of real knowledge workers' real-life problems and challenges. Our technology "sees" everything in silicon that is whizzing around the organization. It is an umbrella application that covers everything going on inside the company. It creates a dashboard for your job and shows you your calendar, your assignments, your reference materials, your documents, your e-mail, and so on. It tracks your time, it monitors the programs in which you're involved, it helps enforce process by allowing you to check off steps, it enables collaboration, and when you seek knowledge it will go into every nook and cranny and pull together everything about a program, entirely in context. It's all in context because everything the knowledge workers do is tagged with a simple program code so that it's all attached to the single opportunity, initiative, or program, whether it's a *Word* document, a letter, an e-mail, a progress chart, a budget, or a threaded discussion. The more disciplined the organization is in enforcing project management and creating realistic updates about progress, the more valuable the knowledge-management tool becomes in analyzing what's gone wrong or right, or identifying the bottlenecks or the key value-adds that are the secret of success.

This type of enterprise-wide knowledge management, combined with business processes, is able to improve the way knowledge is used throughout the entire organization. It gives everyone in the organization a way of communicating, which improves the way they work.

Enterprise software is magnificent at capturing explicit knowledge and presenting it for managers to see. You can cut the deck however you like, summoning all the material about a program, searching by categories for everything an organization has done in a functional domain, searching by an individual's work, and even getting background on his or her functional experience, training, and so on. In the example above, the market analysis and risk analysis documents would have been attached to the individual programs from the beginning. They would have been sitting there when the other consultants went in to see how the sluggers conducted their business with those clients. Soon, everybody would pick up on those additional steps, and they would be incorporated in everyone's business processes.

Tacit Knowledge: Managing Mojo and Serendipity

Tacit knowledge, in contrast to explicit knowledge, is all the stuff that is ephemeral, experience based, or situational. It's the know-how or the expertise that turns mere employees into knowledge workers. It's finesse, it's timing, it's cleverness, it's skill as opposed to competency, it's mojo. It's that sixth sense about work involving people or the presenting or manipulating of information that leaves the also-rans moaning: What's he got that I don't? It comes from genes, from being unusually alert, from making connections and processing patterns well, and from good old-fashioned experience. You can't teach a person tacit knowledge (although you might be able to lead a person to actually create that knowledge for him- or herself). You can't store tacit knowledge in a database per se.

We would argue that tacit knowledge is actually an organization's sweet spot. The reason Rhonda is a process wonk is that you don't want people wasting brain cycles on reinventing the wheel, coming up with their own private "standards," or re-creating some of the other basic elements of your business every time they start something new. Process takes care of that. Then, their brains are freed up to let their tacit knowledge rip.

You can access and assist the sharing of tacit knowledge for the good of your company in two ways. The first is using a smart system that lets your people tag even informal communication, unusual memos, e-mails, and so on with project codes that effortlessly herd bits of knowledge into an appropriate context. Let's say you took a training course that you later realized had prepared you particularly well to analyze those process issues at the Alaskan pipeline site. You probably were asked for an evaluation of that course. In the context of an enterprise-based system like ours you could code that evaluation with the Alaskan pipeline project, and suddenly someone researching what he or she needed to know before tackling a similar project would see it and better understand the preparation he or she needed. Or let's say a customer in one company provided some important data that helped your product developers implement a special feature in a software program. The customer's advice and help consisted of a single e-mail. Tagging that to the project produces a valuable clue to what later developed—without diverting anyone from his or her normal tasks to deliberately enter it into the system.

The other way is by promoting collaboration. Writing down tacit knowledge results in only a pale shadow of what it really is. The thought pattern and experience of the person who's developed the knowledge is important, too. In a perfect universe, every manager wishes every employee on his or her team had all the finely honed, tacit knowledge of every single other person on the team, right? Consider, for example, being able to access accurate knowledge about customer sensitivities in other parts of the world to certain marketing messages. There might be hints of this in e-mails and memos, but the real nitty-gritty knowledge asset here resides in a live person who's lived and worked in different countries. We need that person to actually teach people about the cultures of the South Pacific or Europe. Should we use a rock star spokesperson in Fiji? Will emphasizing a product's low price fly in Germany? These aren't yes-no discussions. Instead, what's needed is expertise in nuance and context and rationale, expertise that is conveyed through conversation that enables the group to add this knowledge to its own in a meaningful way.

Collaboration means efficient communication of the right ideas. It means putting what you know on the table and getting input from people who know something else or something more. Ultimately the work is richer and better for that sharing. Collaboration implies teamwork—whether the teams are formal, virtual, or just individual employees who may call upon other individual employees for help on an as-needed basis. The ideal knowledge management system works in this context by folding collaboration tools inside a larger scheme. By doing so, it also can capture some of the direct fruits of collaboration like e-mails and discussion threads and group to-do lists. In this way, you can begin to capture both explicit and tacit information in context. Very exciting stuff.

Smart Teamwork

Strictly speaking, teams tend to work in sequential or collaborative modes, or in a combination of the two.

In a sequential mode, work is broken down so that each person can work on his or her part individually, then pass it on to the next person. Tacit knowledge tends to be acquired but often not shared while the work is being accomplished sequentially. Collaborative work, in contrast, is true teamwork—that is, everyone is working together in concert. This is the type of work best suited to sharing tacit knowledge. Some people mistakenly think that sequential work is more efficient. They reason that, if work flowed efficiently from one person to the next, everyone would be busy, and everyone's time and talents would be utilized 100 percent. Whether the workflow is sequential or collaborative is really a matter of the type of work being accomplished. If one person, with no input from anyone else, can complete a process step, then the work should be considered sequential.

In more strictly collaborative work, formal meetings, hallway conversations, informal discussions, and heated debates all increase your organization's tacit knowledge. The important thing is that each step, whether sequential or collaborative, be viewed as a step in the business process that eventually is written down, accepted, and followed. Captured communications around those interactions, properly tagged to a specific project (that is, meeting notes, e-mailed agendas, transcripts, and so on), all belong in the overall project context.

If you're trying to tell if your organization needs more collaboration mojo, ask yourself these questions:

- Does your organization typically stumble time and time again on the same ordinary activities (perhaps closing the quarter's books, getting approvals on requisitions, getting accurate sales forecasts)?
- Are these ordinary activities critical to the operation of your organization?
- Are you dependent on one or two key people to perform these activities?
- If these people are absent, does all hell break loose?

If you answer yes to these questions, look for opportunities to add some collaboration. Add review steps to your business processes. Encourage input, encourage discussions, and encourage interaction. Provide frequent opportunities for your people to get together, within the context of the business process, to complete their tasks. Some of the opportunities may be formal, others informal. The New York investment bank Bear Stearns, for example, utilizes formal collaboration mechanisms such as managerial and review boards, says John Elliott, a managing director. The company's architecture review board, for example, was originally an operational meeting designed to gather status data. Over several months, it became clear that it was a powerful mechanism for communication and collaboration too, and it became so useful in knowledge sharing that it changed its charter and morphed into a discussion forum for sharing tacit knowledge. People now use this meeting to discuss interesting projects and to allow people to notify everyone else about what is going on in their areas. In this way, cross-organizational boundaries can be breached, and tacit knowledge from one organizational area can quickly be adopted by others.

Collaborative meetings are longer than meetings that have simpler communication requirements, but much more work gets done. As a knowledge manager, resist the temptation to bark out "Take it offline" every time the discussion broadens.

Elements of Advanced (And Thus Simplified) Knowledge Management

A knowledge system to support knowledge workers needs to have the following capabilities:

- Store and update explicit knowledge
- Enable sharing of tacit knowledge
- Maintain a historical record of knowledge work

Store and Update Explicit Knowledge

An effective knowledge management solution allows knowledge workers to use explicit knowledge in the course of their daily activities. As they learn new things, the knowledge workers update the information in their knowledge store with minimal effort. Ideally the update will require nothing more than directing documents or data they have already created in the course of working. To accomplish this, the knowledge store should be integrally linked with their business process systems.

In an integrated program, explicit knowledge such as processes, process steps, guidelines, and templates are also captured as they're created. As the knowledge worker becomes more experienced and is exposed to different situations, he or she will likely run across additional pieces of explicit knowledge that can then be uploaded back into the knowledge store. This will improve the quality of the explicit knowledge in the knowledge store.

For instance, take the example we used earlier in the chapter for the slugger and laggard graphic designers. To take maximum advantage of the sluggers' presentation process, their actual process, not just the deliverables, should be available in the system. To capture this work, the system provides a process template that an employee checks off as he or she moves through the work, a constantly updated to-do list that becomes a historical record of how the work was done and a process template for the next person.

In this way explicit knowledge is categorized in a knowledge store and can be improved with every use.

Enable Sharing of Tacit Knowledge

It's more important that tacit knowledge be shared than stored. The knowledge store would provide opportunities for the knowledge worker to contact and interact with experts and other coworkers to prompt insight into a new situation. The knowledge store would then be updated with these new experiences via pairing any communication or documents collected in that experience with the explicit knowledge documents of the program. The knowledge store should allow knowledge workers to locate experts who could have insight into their current problem. Knowledge workers could also search the archives for historical data that was similar to their current situation. The knowledge store would then allow the knowledge worker to contact and collaborate with the experts. If an expert could not be found, she could simply collaborate with coworkers to prompt insight and new ideas.

This collaboration actually creates new tacit knowledge. At the end of this experience, the knowledge store will have up-to-date information based on this experience, and it will exist in the form of a work product that had to be created anyway. The knowledge store will also have the knowledge worker's name on its expert list.

For example, a new knowledge worker must prepare a presentation about implementing just-in-time manufacturing in power supply assembly plants located in the northwestern region of the United States. The new knowledge worker doesn't know anything about any of these topics, so he searches the knowledge store to try to find someone who knows something about any of these topics. The new knowledge worker finds Rhonda; they have a long discussion, which the knowledge worker turns into a presentation that Rhonda reviews, modifies, and sends back. The knowledge worker sends this updated presentation to his boss and a few other colleagues, who mark it up, annotate it, and make some further minor changes. The knowledge worker is also able to see, in the knowledge store, all of the information about Rhonda's past engagement at a different northwest power supply assembler. He is able to look over the client engagement agreement, detailed meeting notes, weekly plant schedules, defect lists, engagement plans, and other deliverables from Rhonda's old engagement, providing him additional background information and a deeper understanding of his current position. He makes the presentation to his client. He stores this presentation in the knowledge store, along with all of his other deliverables. The knowledge store now knows that he knows quite a lot about just-in-time manufacturing in power supply assembly plants located in the northwestern region of the United States. And he does. His work has built on Rhonda's, which has been further enhanced by the tacit knowledge they've shared in conversation and collaboration.

A lot of those steps would have been done under any circumstance. But they would rarely have been captured in process or been made available in an integrated way for the next person who comes along. None of these steps adds or removes work, per se, although they should very well limit a lot of bad leads and decisions based on incomplete knowledge, such as modeling an unsuccessful past approach.

Maintain a Historical Record of Knowledge Work

Every program in the organization should be stored in the knowledge store and exist as a code to which information can be attached. Each program should be a collaborative workspace, where all program participants can store their documents. These documents can be anything: deliverables, meeting minutes, e-mail messages, threaded discussions, or any other electronic document that could be stored in a computer system. All work associated with a program can then be handled within the knowledge store. The program area provides the context for the later retrieval and review of these documents.

Similarly, all business processes should be kept in the knowledge store. If a program requires a business process, the process should be loaded into the program in the knowledge store, along with templates for the deliverables, guidelines, or hints for working with the process.

Project management processes should similarly be stored in the knowledge store. Templates for the deliverables for the different project management phases should be loaded into the program in the knowledge store when the program is created.

Progress tracking should be integrated with the knowledge store. Knowledge workers can track progress on any program they should be working on. This updating on actual efforts and new ETCs should in turn update the program schedules automatically.

Completed programs should remain in the knowledge store, along with all of their data: deliverables, plans, schedules, e-mails, and all that other stuff. This is what makes the knowledge store supremely valuable: as a historical record of what the organization did, what it knows, and who knows it. Historical data, in the form of completed activities, programs, projects, and tasks, is what knowledge workers will access when they need guidance on where to find information to prompt new tacit knowledge. They can also look for the actual work that was done in the programs: existing plans, schedules, notes, and other deliverables that they can either reuse outright or review for their good information. These can all be used as the spark to create new tacit knowledge.

If, when working on a program or project, you can seamlessly find and collaborate with others who have worked on similar projects, you will have real synergy. You don't have to log into a separate collaboration system and enter all the information needed to provide context. You do not have to try to reinvent the context, or piece it together from a potentially incomplete deliverables list. The context is already there, surrounding the work you or others have already done. The program charter is there, and the program's schedule and budget are there, along with the business process that was used. All deliverables are in place, and all threaded discussions, notifications, to-do's, and approval steps are noted. If you have a question that cannot be answered by reviewing these things, one that can be answered only by experts with experience in actually doing the work in the program, you can identify them, using the program information, and then send inquiries to them.

You can send these inquiries from within your active project. These inquiries can provide the experts with links back to your project so that they can delve into the details and base their responses on better contextual information. The expert can review the client engagement agreement, detailed meeting notes, weekly schedules, budget revisions, defect lists, engagement plans, and other deliverables. The expert has the opportunity to get more information about the specific problem, and he or she can look at any other deliverables to gain more specific context. It all happens automatically. No need for reinventing the wheel, no need for re-creating anything, no need for filing anything in a separate system; it's all there.

Most work artifacts are useful only for the engagement for which they were created. The energy you expend in cleaning these deliverables and putting them in a separate place usually vastly outweighs the benefit of having them in a repository. The answer, then, is to keep all documents in the place they were born.

Remember the dual challenge here: Plopping a great, big knowledge management system in the middle of your workforce and expecting it to make immature, unmanaged knowledge workers instantly more knowledgeable will not work. Knowledge creation does not just happen. You have to set the stage.

Sadly, not everyone did emerge from kindergarten with a firm grasp on the importance of sharing. You'll need to reinforce its importance in the context of making your organization work better and smarter—and thus, ultimately support each employee's ambitions. Knowledge workers need a framework to recognize, define, store, and reuse explicit knowledge. They need a tool to share tacit knowledge. No matter how great your processes are, no matter how transparent your organization or how well aligned your people's efforts are, you will be ignoring your organization's greatest asset—your people's knowledge—if you do not foster behaviors that improve the ways in which knowledge is created and used.

9

The Diba Diaries

ROM APRIL 1996 until the fall of the same year, Farzad participated in what was, at the time, a novel and even revolutionary use of the Internet: *Upside* magazine asked him to keep a diary of the early days of Diba, the company he and his brother Farid had formed to make software for all the handheld devices called *information appliances* that were starting to appear. Thanks to the Web, the weekly column was an almost-real-time look at the challenges, the triumphs, and the curveballs faced by a startup. They had a very hot technology, and Farzad's candor and accessibility through the Web page diary attracted a lot of attention. By the time the company was sold to Sun in 1997, just 18 months after its founding, Diba had been featured in hundreds of media reports, and Farzad had been on the covers of *Upside* and *Red Herring*.

The diary was a big hit. Farzad would get up to 100 e-mail messages a day from other entrepreneurs and would-be entrepreneurs. Most entrepreneurs are filled with conflicting emotions of overconfidence, exuberance, and terror, and they readily identified with Farzad's experiences. Most of all, they loved reading about one of their own. Farzad became very well known and expectations ran high.

As we both look back on those days now—and it's interesting that Farzad had never actually read all the diary entries in succession before we sat down to do it for this book—we shake our heads at many of the memories, sometimes with a chuckle and a smile, other times with a wince and a grimace.

Diba had a classic, knowledge-worker-driven culture. It was dominated by software developers. It was loaded with high jinks. As managers, Farid and Farzad were impatient and at the time unwilling or unable to get the team properly organized and focused to make the kind of progress they could have. As you read this, the origins of some of our most strongly held beliefs should become quite clear.

The following excerpts are from the actual diaries, which ran as the "Upstart" column on *Upside* online. The triumphs and blunders are in their original form (although we've cut out sections that went into detail about financing or PR strategy that are unrelated to the management of knowledge workers). We annotated the excerpts in spots as well, to provide more perspective.

Upstart

April 2, 1996

Epiphanies come in the weirdest places. Paul's was on the road to Damascus. Newton discovered the theory of gravity supposedly while sitting under an apple tree. Mine came one chilly October day last year while contemplating a herd of Scottish Highlander cows on a relative's "gentleman's" farm in upstate Vermont. My wife's uncle and aunt, a retired American Airlines pilot and a flight attendant, had recently purchased a dozen of these golden-hued, shaggy-haired cows—not for their milk but because they loved the animals' beautiful color. Looking at those cows, seeing the way my in-laws had so boldly color-coordinated their world, inspired in me an urge to take more creative control over my life. It was time, I decided, to start my own company.

> [*Rhonda: See cows, switch jobs. Sounds like something from* The Manchurian Candidate. *But after having been married to him for 13 years, I am used to these epiphanies.*]

For the previous 6 years, I had worked at Oracle Corporation in the "House of Larry," as we liked to call it. And it was a beautiful house indeed; very *shibui* as he would say (Japanese for a concept of beauty based on austerity—simple, yet refined). I had tremendous opportunities for growth and advancement. On that October day, I was the senior vice president of the New Media Division, a 350-person software development organization that was creating Oracle's interactive television, ISDN, and Internet technologies. Not bad for a 31-year-old who had started off as a C programmer in Oracle's Desktop Products Division.

But living in someone else's house, no matter how congenial, isn't the same as having your own home. At the end of the day, you always have to ask permission to move a wall or recarpet a room. And I was tired of all that. So I quit. No drama. No "feigned suicides" to entice them to give me more money or stock options. I simply submitted my resignation and left the company 3 weeks later with little more than a vague notion on which to base a new company. My friends wondered if I was crazy. My wife, Rhonda, was supportive of my need for a new voyage.

[Rhonda: I also had worked at Oracle for 6 years, but I had no problem living in the House of Larry. I thought the walls and carpeting were just fine. But I knew that it was Farzad's decision, not mine, and he had made up his mind. Farzad left a lot of money on the table in the form of unvested stock options. It also seemed as though he was leaving at a promising time in his career. One of the Oracle employees who reported to Farzad couldn't believe he was leaving. He told Farzad that he would do almost anything to have Farzad's position at Oracle, which included lots of access to Larry.]

The only person who was truly overjoyed was my older brother, Farid, who had been telling me every time I got a raise or large bonus that the golden handcuffs were closing tighter and tighter. . . .

The first moments of any new adventure are the most precious and telling. For me, it was recapturing the feeling that work is about having fun; the first moment I realized that there was no one above me saying no to my plans; the knowledge that the culture of this new company was mine to shape and direct. The biggest surprise—and most frightening— was the realization that we had the complete freedom to set whatever business direction we wanted. Like arriving at grocery store without a list, it is a feeling of infinite choice and utter terror about where to begin.

We have now been in business several months. Last Wednesday I cooked lunch in our office kitchen for all the people in the company. I take out trash when it piles up, clean the conference table before important customer meetings, and answer my own telephone. Just last week, I took a long bus ride to downtown Tokyo from the Narita Tokyo Airport after I learned just how expensive the limousine I had so casually taken in the past actually was. It is a long way from my Oracle days. But it is a house of my own. . . .

[Farzad: Those are a couple of scary words—freedom and fun. At the time I was so tired of sitting in meeting after meeting where the good of Oracle was never discussed, only small issues related to the career aspirations of whoever happened to be at the meeting, cast in the buzzword parlance of the day. It was exhilarating to escape that. So much so that I found myself smiling as I took out the trash.]

Family Ties

April 8, 1996

Older brothers often cast long shadows. This was certainly the case with my brother, Farid, who was born 2 years before me and is the cofounder of Diba. Farid was always steady and focused, and he excelled at everything he did, whereas I was easily bored and quickly moved from one idea to the next. He was always at the top of his class. I was too, but for the life of me I couldn't understand why everyone thought school was so important. . . .

We came to the United States from Iran in 1979, at the peak of turmoil in our homeland. Five days after we landed in California, aboard one of the last planes to leave Tehran, the Shah abdicated and all hell broke loose. No one in our family has ever been back since then. I was 14, Farid was 16. We joined our parents and younger sister, who had arrived several months before to find a house, buy a car, and start our new life. During those last months in Iran, we spent most evenings playing backgammon by candlelight during the endless power outages and listening to the gunfire outside our home. . . .

Farid graduated from Stanford with a master's degree in mechanical engineering and went to work at HP. My junior year he advised me that software was "where the action was," so I added a degree in computer science to my mechanical engineering curriculum. He stayed at HP 4 more years, which included a 1-year master's fellowship at Cornell. I joined GE's nuclear power division, moved to Tandem, and from there to Oracle.

[Rhonda: Farzad neglects to mention that he was only 19 when he graduated with two bachelor's degrees, one in computer science, one in mechanical engineering. He is one credit away from getting a master's degree, one of the few things he never finished. I have a bachelor's degree in nuclear engineering, which really puts a damper on some social conversations. I also have an MBA, which is more socially acceptable.]

I'll never forget the afternoon 4 years ago when Farid told me he was quitting his job to form his own company, which eventually became Wavetron Microsystems. He had $2000 in the bank, a $3000 monthly mortgage, and absolutely no idea what this company would do. I had just been promoted to vice president at Oracle, in charge of a huge project to reposition the company's line of server tools. My father said to me, "Don't worry, some day you'll be successful like Farid." Farid and I both laughed. . . .

When I finally called Farid last year—at 10:50 P.M. on October 17, 1995—to announce that I was resigning from Oracle, he was overjoyed. In fact, he was so happy he decided then and there that he would sell his company, and we would go into business together. To do what, we weren't sure at the time. Two months later we formed Diba. . . . We both believe that starting our own company is the greatest adventure in life, that treating our employees well is the key to our success, and that agility and flexibility when responding to change is our greatest strategic advantage. . . .

[Farzad: As you'll soon see, "treating people well" came to represent something very different to me than I envisioned it in the early days of Diba. Then, I think I saw it as removing bureaucracy and encouraging people to bond and have fun. Today, I simply see it as trying to manage people in as honest a fashion as possible: rewarding them when you realize how valuable they are—not waiting until they're fed up and ready to leave; getting rid of people who aren't cutting it, rather than allowing employees to die slow deaths. I still believe that agility and flexibility when responding to change are critical. What's changed for me, however, is the realization that you can be most flexible only when you completely understand where you are and where you want to be. It's that transparency thing. You need good information to respond appropriately to new opportunities and challenges, not just guts and a willingness to make big, bold decisions quickly.]

Chasing the Money

April 16, 1996

Farid and I were more fortunate than most entrepreneurs in that we were able to obtain several million dollars in financing—enough to cover our first year of operations—from a large corporate investor within our first week of business. The week that I announced my resignation at Oracle, I was on a plane with my wife and son, headed to the East Coast. The colorful CEO of a highly profitable software company was sitting just in front of us. He and I had participated together on speaker panels at several industry conferences and had briefly done business together at Oracle. I was feeling grumpy at the prospect of a long plane flight and nodded a quick hello. To my surprise, he turned around 30 minutes into the flight and said: "If you ever decide to start your own company, make sure that you call me, I'd like to make an investment."

Five days later, having resigned from Oracle, Farid and I were on a plane to that CEO's company headquarters, where we presented our business concept—exactly 12 slides—to his executive committee. Twenty-four hours later we had a verbal commitment for enough money to fund our first year. We were in a state of complete shock. . . .

Our First Home

April 22, 1996

Several years ago, my wife, Rhonda, and I renovated our house in the hills of Monte Sereno, just north of San Jose. It had begun life in the 1930s as an 800-square-foot summer cottage for a San Francisco family—and had seen happier days. We had just gotten married and didn't have a lot of money, so we tackled the initial demolition ourselves. From that experience, I came away with many cuts and bruises, and a newfound appreciation for the importance of that part of the house I had largely ignored before—the foundation. As Rhonda and I learned, you can change anything if you have solid concrete underneath.

> *[Rhonda: One of the things that Farzad does not mention is that we started renovating this house without a clear understanding of what we wanted. We did not have blueprints. We did not have an architect. We did not have permits. When we hired a contractor, we did not have a contract. I use the term "we" loosely. Obviously the Process Queen was not intimately involved with most of these activities. After coming home from a hardware store with paint cans and brush in hand, I was surprised to turn around one day as I started cooking dinner only to find that Farzad had begun to paint the wall even before cleaning off the countertops, even before taping, even before sanding, or even cleaning the walls and cabinets.]*

When we started Diba, one of the first priorities Farid and I had was constructing an infrastructure. We knew that this process would be time consuming and expensive, but we were adamant that we wouldn't repeat the mistake made by many software startups, whose successes quickly overrun their ability to take advantage of them. . . .

Building a Product
April 29, 1996

Watching a startup grow is very much like watching a baby mature. It's a process of continual change. I was always astonished at how quickly my son David, now 4 years old, seemed to grow and change. He would be crawling one morning and tottering about that evening. This kind of rapid change—both for a baby and a new company—is a sign of good health. As one investment banker we are talking with said, "Beware of companies who, a year after being founded, are still trying to implement the exact same technology they began with." . . .

So is the product concept we launched today the same one Farid and I began with 6 months ago? Not by a long shot. Back in late 1995, the initial technology we at Diba hoped to create was not nearly as crystal clear. When I left Oracle, I literally had no idea that I would create a software platform for what our partners now tell us may usher in the next revolution in consumer electronics products. In fact, three of our earliest employees—Mark Moore, Stuart Read, and Joe Gillach—joined us before the company had been named or the product or business model had been conceived. We joked that we were all "drinking the Kool Aid"—but weren't even sure what flavor it was supposed to be!

The only thing we agreed on at our founding is that Diba would have two guiding missions: to create a business that would bring the power of computing to average users and to have fun. As we examined and rejected various business and technology ideas, these two principles would remain the North Star by which we steered our company. . . . It wasn't until we were in business 3 weeks, in mid-December, that we hit upon the idea of creating a software platform for a broad family of information appliances. The idea for IDEAs (our favorite pun here at Diba) was born after several meetings with Japanese and Korean consumer electronics companies. These folks had invested in set-top box technology for the interactive TV market, which has since proven slow to emerge. Again and again we heard consistent stories about their strong interest in embedding more powerful computing power in their electronics and appliance products—and their equally strong distrust of doing so in cooperation with established PC manufacturers, whom they view as potential competitors.

The sum, then, of hearing a well-defined set of requirements from an eager set of partners (consumer electronics companies), coupled with the benefit of having a large company (Oracle) evangelizing the need for a new generation of computing devices (albeit with a poor solution to the problem) helped crystallize our vision for bringing "more information to more people."

Someone once said that no force in nature is as powerful as an idea whose time has come.

[Farzad: I still can't read these words without a bit of cringing. The time had not come. Although we would later sell Diba to Sun for a multiple on the invested capital in the business, fact is, no product was ever introduced based on our technology. The idea behind Diba is just as relevant—and just as nonexistent—today as it was in 1996. The biggest single mistake we made with Diba was an exaggerated sense of urgency. We ran pell-mell without good visibility into the developing but still nascent market for info appliances. Time is not always of the essence.

One thing we did right here, however, was spend lots of time discussing requirements with customers. We weren't trying to jam engineering down anybody's throat. We had accepted that the customer pays the salaries, the bills, and everything else.]

Molding the Diba Culture

May 6, 1996

Being old Silicon Valley hands, none of the Diba management team were under any illusion that we could deliberately dictate or mandate a culture for our new company. That is not to say that we didn't attempt to plant the seeds we hoped would grow into a unique culture—one that reflected our personal and business values.

Our second week in business, we wrote a company manual that outlined not only our employee benefits and business operating policies but also spelled out the values we wanted to instill in our company culture. First and foremost, we wrote about our desire for Diba to be "about having fun" and our commitment that Diba be a "kinder and gentler" place to work. Having all come from companies where aggressiveness often reaped greater rewards (at least in the short term) than teamwork, we were determined to promote a different model for success. . . .

One of the earliest events in our company history, and one that has had a remarkable influence on our culture, occurred over the New Year's weekend. We were scheduled to take possession of our offices that following Tuesday, January 2. Without any planning or prompting, all 12 members of the company showed up early Saturday morning to begin cleaning up and wiring our building. Even more remarkably, everyone showed up with a box of doughnuts—many from the same bakery around the corner. . . . [This] established a precedent that everyone, regardless of background or position, pitches in when an important job needs to be done. Second, it demonstrated that the management team is far from infallible and is open to suggestions and help. I remember watching with amusement as Patrick Coleman, one of our young developers, taught Greg Wolff, our VP of product marketing, how to use a punch-down tool, and Andy Lloyd—who hadn't yet even officially hired on as our marketing assistant—showed Joe Gillach, our chief operating officer, how to string wiring through the false ceiling. . . .

Serendipity has played a large role in shaping our culture. These unexpected events have provided much laughter and, through constant retelling, are quickly becoming Diba "legends." Like the time when we accidentally served "Spike" coffee to a group of Korean visitors. Spike is the favorite beverage of choice among our developers because it is super-caffeinated (much like Jolt cola). Our office manager, Susan, unwittingly made a huge pot of Spike, which our unsuspecting Korean visitors quickly guzzled down. Ten minutes later, the conference room erupted into a heated frenzy of discussion. By the end of the morning, our visitors were embracing us and literally jumping up and down in excitement. We now refer to any successful customer meeting as having been "Spiked"— although we are now careful to only serve Starbucks to our visitors.

Finally, there are the Nerf guns. One of our developers brought in a Nerf machine gun that fires 10 Nerf bullets (soft foam) in rapid succession. In what they claim was pure self-defense, all the other developers immediately went out and purchased similar Nerf weapons—so many that our office now resembles a Nerf warehouse. Just last week, a delivery man asked whether Diba is a toy company. . . .

Am I happy with the culture that has arisen here at Diba? Almost without exception, yes. I wish—and will probably always wish—that people would communicate more with each other. I am disappointed that we have been unable to hire a single female engineer. And I wish we could justify doing something as a company for our community. In fact, at our first management committee meeting, we discussed our desire to donate money or time to a local charity, but we decided it was more responsible to wait until we had generated our first profits rather than give away the funds committed by our investor—and which we would surely need in order to grow. . . .

[*Farzad: In the early days of Diba we had some very positive bonding experiences, like helping wire the company office together. I would encourage and welcome them again in a heartbeat. Group meals were a fun way for a small group to relax some of the inevitable tension and pressure that builds during marathon coding sessions and stressful technical challenges. But I also get a small shiver when I look back at the advent of the Nerf gun wars, for example. Here I see myself giving in to the culture and celebrating exactly the kind of thing that was beginning to worry me.*]

[*Rhonda: My perspective was that Diba was able to attract and retain very intelligent and highly skilled engineers. I think that many of these engineers did some of their best work at Diba. The solutions they came up with were incredibly creative and innovative. In the early days, exuberance in work as well as play made Diba a very special place to be. As corny as it sounds, people really cared about their work, as opposed to their place on the corporate ladder. People cared about the product, as opposed to how this job was going to look on their résumé.*

The culture started as "work hard, play hard, do cool things." But it became "mumble, mumble, play hard, do cool things." Playing with Nerf guns became more important than writing code. As products matured, ideas became solidified, and customers were signed, there was no balancing between culture and work. There was no understanding that work exists because of these customers. The feeling was that we work because it's fun, and customers are sometimes inconvenient. So, when management, including Farzad, tried to gently steer the organi-

zation in the right customer-focused direction, some employees felt betrayed. "I thought you were hiring me for my creativity, not my ability to code for 8 hours." Some of the engineers turned sullen and started sabotaging efforts to steer the company in the right direction, toward customers and profitability. There was a serious maturity gap here, one Farzad vowed we'd never allow to develop again.]

Standing on the Shoulders of Giants—Our Developers
May 13, 1996

It is sad, but frequently true, that the people most deserving of credit often receive the least attention, especially when it comes to attention from the press. Surveying the phenomenal coverage we have received over the past several weeks—from our company's unveiling to last week's partnership announcement with Zenith—Farid and I are a bit disconcerted that, as founders, our pictures appear in print, when so much of Diba's success is due to our development team. A statesman once said that it is easy to appear tall when you are standing on the shoulders of giants. . . .

Originally, our staff was constructed from individuals with whom we had strong, long-standing business and personal relationships, dating from before the conception of Diba. From this core group of colleagues and friends, our ranks expanded, through the enthusiasm of Farid and myself, and that of our initial staff.

In the beginning, word of mouth and the power of persuasion were our best recruiting tools as we set out to develop a top-notch team. For example, our current team of graphics engineers worked together on NASA's computational fluid dynamics visualization software project, designing software for the space shuttle. We like to joke that our developers really are rocket scientists. . . .

Keeping this setup running smoothly is the Herculean task of Mark Moore, the head of the development team and one of the best engineering managers in the valley. Mark had to implement a tightly structured development process, which isn't always welcome by developers, who like to think of themselves as artists and chafe at anything that resembles bureaucracy. Most days Mark can be found working side by side with his team, head down, coding. Otherwise, he spends his time interviewing candidates and presenting Diba's technical approach to potential partners.

And the unsung heroes? The Diba engineers. Their technical qualifications are straightforward: All of them can quickly produce clean, elegant code or hardware. It's their nontechnical characteristics that are more difficult to describe.

They are all entrepreneurs at heart—a necessity in an early-stage startup. They share an almost messianic passion for the technology we are developing. When asked to describe their products, they begin with words like "hot," "big," and "supercool"—only later bothering to describe functionality. . . . Our developers have amazing physical endurance. Most work 14-hour days, a minimum of 6 days a week. In fact, the team working on our TV Web browser technology just came off a 21-day solid work stint. As you might imagine, niceties like shaving and laundry fell by the wayside. They also have cast-iron stomachs, as exhibited by the wreckage left in the refrigerator after their all-nighters—pizza with the works, caramel sauce, chili, and half-eaten rib carcasses. . . .

Without question, our engineers are a colorful group: Dave, counted on for his even temper and thoughtfulness. He turns beet-red and starts giggling after half a drink at our Friday evening beer fests. . . . Brandon, a *Friends* TV show addict. He was recently shot point-blank in the forehead with a Nerf gun by a girlfriend, leaving a 2-inch scar, at our Spring Fling party. . . . Patrick, resident instigator. . . . You can be sure that when betting is taking place—to see who can roll the big red ball into Farid's office without touching the door frame—Patrick was somehow involved. . . . Scott, our resident coffee aficionado. . . . Tom, the original perpetrator of our Nerf gun tradition . . .

[Rhonda: The original diary had even more detail about the idiosyncrasies of these developers. What's interesting to me now is the one person who was the most intensely focused on the product then, Mark Moore, is not described by his wardrobe or television show preferences but for his expertise in development. He is the SVP of development at Niku.]

From quirks to code, when Farid and I stand in front of our customers, we tell them with confidence that we have the best development team in the valley.

[Farzad: When it came to managing these guys we were subconsciously afraid of turning off their energy, and so we gave them a lot of mixed

messages. We were like "Jock" managers: Just do it. At the same time, we would occasionally become furious that they hadn't read our minds or anticipated some problem that only careful study and a much more coordinated effort could have provided. It was becoming an example of leave people alone and good things will not happen. . . . The Nerf guns were supposed to compensate for the badgering.

At Niku, Rhonda ran development, and the attitude couldn't have been more different. We'd get a team together, and Rhonda would insist we spend the next 3 months figuring out what exactly we were going to do before we started to do it. At first it drove me crazy! We didn't have time for this!]

[Rhonda: He almost had a stroke! Even the developers, some of whom had known Farzad longer than I had, were apoplectic at some of my ideas. You would have thought that I was asking them to take public transit to work.]

[Farzad: Then you look at the results. Niku 6, our flagship program, came in on time to the day, with fewer errors and problems—and no nasty badgering. Process was the way to go; aligning goals with projects was the way to go. Even more relevant to this discussion is that at Diba, Mark Moore operated without much process. Once Rhonda brought in process to Niku, Mark was able to use this, and everything worked better. It unleashed his development genius to work in a more accountable, organized way and require that from his reports. Now I realize success on the product front can compensate for the Nerf guns.]

Matchmaker, Matchmaker: Partnerships
May 20, 1996

Many people compare working with customers and business partners to a marriage. Once joined, business partners are stuck with each other, for better or worse, and divorce is often painful, expensive, and humiliating. At Diba, we are fortunate to be in the honeymoon stage with our partners, having only recently signed contracts with them to build Diba-based information appliances. Arriving at the altar, though, entailed an enormous amount of effort by both sides, and it took many unpredictable turns along the way. . . .

We fell into a trap common to many startups: We overdisclosed in an attempt to prove our technology and company were real. I wince when recalling one meeting where we spent 4 hours briefing six vice presidents from a major U.S. electronics company on every detail of our technology and business model. At the end of our presentation, we asked them to tell us about their plans. Their senior executive responded by saying, "We intend to make products very similar to yours." With that, they concluded the meeting and we learned a valuable and painful lesson in moderating our eagerness.

The second lesson we learned came from our attempts to license technology from a local vendor. Although this company had the exact technology we needed, we couldn't get it to provide us with business terms. We couldn't seem to locate anyone to authorize a deal. It was extremely frustrating, since we had made it clear we were willing to agree to any reasonable terms. From this we learned the value of a standard price list or pricing mechanism, a standard letter of agreement and business contract, and the ability to respond quickly when a customer asks for business terms. Nothing is more frustrating to a potential customer than a brilliant technology story bogged down by an incoherent business model.

Growing Pains

May 27, 1996

One of the early and most difficult decisions we faced at Diba was how fast to grow. In an industry and a valley where the "grow, grow, grow" mantra is deafening (and often drowns out the smaller voice of good sense), we knew that we had no choice but to increase Diba's size and visibility. The question was simply how fast and over what period of time. Startups typically adopt one of two approaches to growth. The first is often termed *constrained growth*. Constrained growth is predictable and relatively comfortable—an approach that many companies have successfully adopted but one that we quickly realized was out of place in our all-or-nothing culture.

The second option, which we fully embraced (though not without some trepidation), was what we call a *go-for-broke* approach to growth. In this scenario, we hire to meet demand—after signing up sufficient partners to ensure a viable business and large market opportunity. Having determined that the market for our technology is a magnitude greater than we initially suspected, we are moving full steam ahead. . . . Growing Diba at this rate will increase the possibility of making more mistakes, needing more money, and swamping our existing infrastructure. I once heard an executive explain how "scale" (size) issues have the power to radically transform simple problems into relatively unrecognizable monsters. He used the analogy of a chef baking a cake. When a chef is creating 1 cake, his or her concerns are straightforward and intuitive—are there two eggs in the refrigerator, is the oven lit, and should it be a chocolate or lemon cake? In contrast, a professional chef baking 500 cakes each day has an entirely different set of concerns—which farmer can reliably supply the fresh eggs and butter, is there sufficient warehouse space to store the flour and sugar, and will he or she be able to hire enough assistant bakers?

Similarly, as our growth has increased to the level of one developer hire a week, our challenges have changed. The predictable things began to fall apart first. We were forced to hire a full-time receptionist to answer our constantly ringing main telephone line, despite an earlier vow to hire no one but developers for the next several months. . . . Most of our office spaces are now doubled up, with plans for tripling up many spaces after we hire five more people. We even subjected ourselves to the indignity of installing a meeting and calendaring system, which had been fervently resisted because of the largely unproductive "meetings" cultures of our former companies. It was tough to outgrow the early days when people's calendars were less full and scheduling a meeting was as simple as wandering down the hallway.

[Rhonda: Many companies operate under the assumption that they should spend to grow, as opposed to earn to grow. Concentrating mostly on the product, and the technology to create it, has made them overlook the challenge of developing a balanced organization.]

Some of the growth strains have been less predictable and turned out to be more important and difficult to solve. For example, our biggest task 3 months ago was to sign up a variety of consumer-electronics partners to use our technology in the creation of new information appliances. Now that we have several partners aboard (Zenith and two yet to be announced), our challenge is to provide focused account management in order to keep pace with product definition and comarketing opportunities. . . . Another sticky challenge caused by our rapid growth is in the area of hiring. Not so much in finding well-qualified people but in the area of "fit." In our early days, every person in the company interviewed a prospective new hire—for both their technical competence and for their fit with the emerging Diba culture. After a candidate left, we discussed whether the person had that (largely undefinable) "Dibaness" that would make them a happy and accepted member of our tribe.

Initially, we valued enthusiasm, boundless energy, and devil-may-care risk taking—those characteristics we considered essential for an early-stage startup. We still look for these qualities, but we are adding more people who bring a certain maturity and dignity.

[Farzad: This may be my earliest recorded acknowledgment of the need for adult supervision.]

Am I thrilled with how quickly, and relatively smoothly, we have been able to grow Diba? Absolutely! I confess that I will miss the small, family-like atmosphere that characterized the early phase of our company. Many of us happily escaped large companies because we found their size inhibited our ability to be creative and have fun. Thus far we have successfully avoided the trappings of a big company and fully intend to keep this place from losing its sense of fun and adventure. Like a person's first home, we recognize the sentimental attachment we have to our first months of operation, but we are happy and excited by the prospect of moving to a much bigger house.

Sizing Up the Competition

June 3, 1996

One of the first questions potential partners and press ask is, "Who is your competition?" . . . When Diba is viewed broadly as a "software platform" company, the field of potential competitors includes companies like Microsoft, Sun, Oracle, and Apple. When viewed more narrowly as an "information appliance software platform" company—the view we have chosen internally—the answer to the competitors question is no one, at least not yet. We have discovered that potential customers, press, and bankers aren't comfortable with a company that has no competitors, especially a small startup littered with Nerf guns. On the surface, it sounds arrogant or suggests that we haven't done our homework. As a result, by default, we have fallen back on the broader perspective when identifying our competition. . . .

So, when it comes to pinpointing the competition, we have adopted what Farid calls the "HP Way"—that is, we never mention competitors unless specifically asked about them. We would rather focus on what we are doing and how Diba can best partner with customers. When asked about a particular competitor, we try to stick to the facts and avoid personal or unfair criticism. After all, many of us proudly worked for these same large companies and we intend, with any luck, to be among their ranks one day.

[Farzad: One of our reader friends who helped with comments and suggestions on this book pointed out that we touch on virtually every aspect of business but one—how competitors fit into the management challenge. I believe that every minute you spend worrying or fretting about your competitors, you miss out worrying about how well you're serving your customers. The latter is far more important—I believed it then, and I believe it now.]

Working with the Press

June 10, 1996

Since the coverage of Diba began, we have also come to appreciate the volatility that excessive press attention can bring to a small business. Press coverage has a certain magnifying effect sort of like going public, from a financial perspective. Greater scrutiny means you receive more applause when things go well, like our recent announcement with Zenith. We are also aware that it can mean harsher coverage if we stumble in the future.

We have been lucky to work with some of the best reporters in the business—people who are well informed, are good listeners, ask intelligent and thoughtful questions, and have the courtesy (when time permits) to allow us to fact-check their articles. Overall, although it has proven to be an immense amount of work, our interactions with the press have been both personally and for Diba a highly positive experience.

[Farzad: Although the press coverage and attention Diba got helped it in many ways and was right for the times, I took the opposite approach with Niku. Good press does help with recruiting, but it is also a big distraction and can get people way off track as they worry too much about what people who really aren't stakeholders think about incomplete information or about products they haven't seen yet.]

Week in the Life of Diba
June 18, 1996

A number of readers have written to ask what a typical day is like at Diba. I thought this was an interesting request—I often wonder what daily life is like at other startups. So, for the week of June 5, I jotted down the major (and minor) events to try to provide a feel for the texture of our hectic days here at Diba.

The big accomplishment for the week was hiring 11 new developers, who will begin work over the next 3 weeks. The office was consumed all week with interviewing potential hires, issuing offer letters, and answering questions about health benefits and 401(k) plans (yes, we have one). We snagged two fantastic engineers from Apple's next-generation OS project, *Copland*. Several other developers were referred to us by recruiters, but the balance came, as usual, from personal contacts. We even resorted to offering a $5000 sign-on bonus for anyone joining during the month of June in order to grease the skids. By the beginning of July, the Diba family will have grown to over 40 people, from 11 just 4 months ago!

We spent $25 on a case of beef jerky (the latest food obsession) for the development team, who promptly ate all of it in 2 days. Despite the indigestion (and beef jerky breath) that ensued, they clamored for more, prompting us to institute a $50-a-month jerky allowance and an official rationing plan. Mutterings about "management's indifference to their dietary needs" can still be heard around the cappuccino machine.

Working with our lawyers at Wilson, Sonsini, Goodrich & Rosati, we finalized the term sheet for a Series B preferred stock sale. We have numerous commitments to invest in Diba, mostly from companies who are licensing our technology. We will begin receiving the first cash in the bank by the end of June. I get a rush when I see how much the value of the company has increased in such a short time. We also met with two investment banks interested in taking us public. It is nice to be the customer for a change.

Farid, Joe Gillach, Stuart Read, and I fielded 28 press and analyst interviews, ranging from *CBS Morning News* (broadcasting a profile on Diba later this month) to *BusinessWeek* (publishing a cover story on June 17, 1996, on information appliances), to the *London Financial Times* and the *Nikkei Techno Frontier* newsletter. Our favorite interview highlighted the Diba kitchen for San Francisco radio station KBLX's weekly food and cooking show. . . .

We hosted nine major customer meetings. Our three conference rooms, which once seemed an extravagance, are now in continuous use. Farid and I love seeing people in suits coming and going (many we don't know or recognize)—a sign that the team doesn't need us involved in every decision anymore.

Farid and Tim Stoutamore, one of our crack developers, were in charge of Wednesday's office lunch. The menu included Swedish meatballs and rice (a big hit), garlic bread, and brownies with both chocolate and vanilla ice cream. What about green, leafy vegetables? As Farid would say, "We don't believe in salad!" . . .

We instituted the first speed limit for what is affectionately known as the "Tour de Diba." The Tour consists of individual time trials (the current record of 26.45 seconds is held by Ted Wong, a product manager) whereby a contestant rides a mountain bike through the entire Diba office without touching a wall or the floor with his or her feet. Unfortunately, being a highly competitive bunch, our folks were attempting to maneuver this obstacle course at faster and faster speeds, causing damage to the wall plaster and terrifying visitors unlucky enough to step into the hallway (the home stretch) as a time trial was concluding. Races are no longer allowed during customer visits, and contestants are required to touch up any paint damage, neither of which seems to have dampened the enthusiasm for the sport.

We hosted a celebration dinner for eight Korean developers and businesspeople who spent the week finalizing the technical and business details on a contract to use our technology. After an exhausting week of negotiations and due diligence, everyone was ready to have fun and toast our new relationship. We can't wait to announce this latest deal in July! . . .

Stuart Read met with the first participants in the Diba Developer Program. This program is designed to help independent software developers create applications using our technology.

Other events of note: We set up our first non-California office—a sales office outside Austin, Texas; ordered Diba T-shirts and business cards for incoming employees; increased our janitorial services from 3 to 5 days a week; and watered the plants.

And—drumroll please—we received our first partner payment $120,000 for Diba technology. We framed a copy of the check and happily put it in the bank. We like to joke that we have now generated more revenue than many companies that have recently issued IPOs!

Looking back over this list, I can attest that this is a fair example of Diba life during any given week. Important events like signing new contracts or hiring new developers are interspersed with the trivial and mundane but oh-so-necessary tasks required to keep a business up and running. To this mix is added a liberal dose of fun—bike races, food fads, the purchase of new toys—which make the long hours and enormous deadline pressures bearable. It is a crazy existence, but one I wouldn't trade for anything in the world.

Every Rose Has Its Thorns

June 25, 1996

To honor the commitment I made in my first column to share the bad with the good, I offer some of the more notable goofs that have happened in our first 6 months of business. No doubt the investment bankers currently swarming around Diba will cringe at these revelations, but as Farid is so fond of saying, "What the hell."

One of the most significant mistakes we made early on was the result of not having conducted a trademark search on our most important product name, *IDEA*. As you may have noticed, we stopped using the *IDEA* acronym (interactive digital electronic appliance) about a month ago, after we were alerted by a series of threatening legal letters from a company that had trademarked the term years earlier. Farid and I originally came up with the idea of using "IDEA" (one of our favorite puns) on the eve of our first press tour—just as our collateral materials were being finalized and sent to the printer. Not having time to do a trademark search, we included the name in all our literature and hoped for the best, which was not long-lasting. Unfortunately, by the time we were forced to abandon the name, we had already spent considerable time promoting it, including designing an IDEA logo for use on future product packaging.

[Farzad: This hurts to read. Startups who have not carefully done a trademark check on their name or a product name have been completely driven out of business after spending considerable money on branding and marketing. This is one of those life-and-death types of process checks you don't have the luxury of ignoring.]

Our inability to accurately forecast company growth has been another ongoing and less-forgiving problem. When we formed Diba in December 1995, we predicted that we would grow to 18 employees by the end of 1996. Based on this forecast, we rented office space, established telephone service, and bought furniture and equipment. Today, only 6 months later, we have 40 employees and anticipate hiring an additional 60 people by the end of the 1996—more than five times our original estimate! Every office in our current building is now tripled up (Farid and I are now sharing an office), our hallways are lined with cubicles, and people are sharing telephone lines. Pac Bell says it needs 60 to 90 days to pull another cable to our building. Only 6 months into a 5-year lease, we are being forced to move to a much larger building. Fortunately, everyone is coping with these overcrowded conditions with good humor and patience. . . . Another glitch, recently uncovered as we put together the final paperwork for closing our second round of investors, is the lack of detailed meeting notes from our monthly board of directors' meetings. Diba's board currently consists of Farid, Fred Ebrahimi, the president of Quark, and myself. Unfortunately, none of us are paperwork people, let alone note-takers, so the details of our meetings haven't been captured for posterity. In any case, our meetings typically consist of a frenzied idea exchange, at the end of which Fred races off to the airport. As we are discovering, documentation is increasingly important as we add investors and approach a public offering. . . .

Many snafus have been less expensive and more humorous. For example, we encountered a problem with our first legal-size mailing envelopes. Just to be different, when we designed these envelopes, we had the return-address block placed in the lower left hand corner rather than the upper left, where it is traditionally found. The first week we sent out these envelopes they mysteriously started coming back. After much investigation, we discovered that the post office uses scanners to scan the mailing address on each envelope. Unfortunately, the scanner was picking up our return address rather than the address of the intended recipient. So rather than being mailed to its rightful destination, these letters were being returned to us. A simple redesign of the envelope corrected the problem, and we ended up with a large supply of scrap paper.

[Rhonda: This entire diary entry is a Process Queen's nightmare. Do what matters. Do it right.]

Just as learning from one's mistakes is supposed to make people wiser, business goofs provide the scars that give a company its character. Or as we like to say at Diba, "What doesn't kill you makes you strong."

What I Did on My Summer Vacation

August 6, 1996

Although not the most important business event of the past month, moving into our new building in Menlo Park last Friday was certainly the emotional highlight, and it came not a moment too soon. You may recall from your introductory college psychology courses what happens to mice when they are subjected to overcrowding. Our former office was zoned to hold 12 people—we figured we could squeeze in 20. By the time the moving trucks arrived, we had shoehorned nearly 40 people into the space. Add constant deadline pressures and one small set of bathrooms, and you begin to get the picture. Things were so tight that we were often forced to hold customer meetings in the kitchen around the Ping-Pong table and interview potential employees in the parking lot.

To say we love our new building is an understatement. It really is a happy, smile-inducing space, in character with our growing company: funky, functional, and fun. Formerly occupied by a manufacturer of wall heaters, the building had been abandoned for 2 years and was, when we first saw it, filthy with accumulated dirt and broken water pipes.

We have added many unique Diba touches. The support poles holding up the 24-foot-high ceilings are being turned into palm trees by affixing artificial palm branches and coconuts to them.

[Farzad: I can practically hear Don Ho playing the ukulele in the background.]

We are surrounding the main area with 12 large Diba flags. And Stuart Read, our resident mountaineer, is installing a rock-climbing area up one of our interior concrete walls (our lawyer is apoplectic about the potential liability issues). And, of course, we have dedicated space for our pool table, the big toy box holding our Nerf guns, and the recently added musical equipment.

[Rhonda: Diba had some wonderful qualities: enthusiastic employees, a really cool idea, terrific technology, and great marketing. It had pizzazz; it had a soul. But it also suffered from a lack of maturity, a lack of accountability, poor follow-through, poor account management, and a lack of clarity in the business plan. Any knowledge manager knows this problem: How can you harness that excitement and enthusiasm yet still make a buck?]

The moment of truth arrived last month—we put our code in the hands of a partner for the first time. We delivered our beta release and documentation to Zenith and several of our yet-to-be announced Japanese and Korean partners. Getting code out the door is always the true test of a development organization, and we are proud to have cleared this first hurdle. . . .

Within this past month, Diba has started to feel like a real company. We are implementing many of the legal, financial, and business processes that we couldn't afford and didn't have the manpower to accomplish previously. Our story is more refined, our target customers more clearly understood, and, most importantly, our technology is progressing as planned.

Now that we are on the eve of finalizing a second round of financing, I am less apprehensive about keeping the doors open (though no less focused on controlling costs) and more concerned about how we will make the transition to a 100-person company that is shipping a product.

Is Diba as fun a place as it was 9 months ago? Absolutely! Even more so on some days. Do I worry as much as I did when we had no customers and only the beginnings of a code base? Just ask my wonderful wife, Rhonda, who has given up trying to count all my gray hairs.

[Farzad: There was to be no "next month." Shortly after this column ran, we began working with investment bankers in expectation of

going public, and all public communications and press interviews had to end. The truth is, the period I wrote about in these diaries was the steady climb up the roller-coaster hill for Diba, and the column ended as we crested the hill. From here on, things became much more difficult and frustrating. Our money was running out, and we didn't have the backing to pursue the public offering as we had hoped. Within a few months, we made the decision to sell Diba to Sun Microsystems. We never disclosed the deal's value, although we returned our investors' money several times over. In that sense, it was a success story.

But it all still seems so surreal to me. It happened so fast and so intensely. We incorrectly perceived ourselves as having no time to think, only to act. There wasn't enough thought at the beginning of the project, not enough even-tempered, intelligent analysis of what we were doing—just a lot of frantic activity. There was nowhere near enough management.

When I think about how excited many of the readers of this column were to see "one of their own" going through all these adventures and presumably picking up some wisdom on how to proceed, the memory is bittersweet. Because we didn't embrace some of the basic attitudes and management principles we're writing about now in this book, all our energy and talent couldn't build a sustainable operation during the mid-1990s—one of the best economic periods in a century. While good management is still not a guarantee of success, I am struck that we are now surviving and are still very optimistic despite sitting in the middle of one of the worst business climates in decades, certainly for our industry. There are still problems. There are always problems. But making sure your organization is accountable and focused on the right things is not a luxury. It's a survival tool.]

The Transparency Payback

W E ARE TRYING to empower executives who aren't content with shrugs and grunts as status reports, who sincerely want to gain control of their workplaces and improve efficiency and productivity. Sometimes, it's because they are thrown into a difficult situation and have the mandate to shake things up and clean things up. Other times, they simply become converted to the power of accountability as a management tool and decide to do an organizational spring cleaning.

In our experience, within 1 to 2 years of a concerted effort to impose the principles of accountability on an organization, visible change occurs in some key areas:

- Interrelated programs are managed as a group, and all are held mutually accountable for success.
- Teamwork is the driving factor, not an individual's efforts.
- Portfolio decisions are based upon objective criteria that are aligned with enterprise strategy.
- The right programs get funded; marginal programs get sidelined.
- Customers work in partnership with the organization.
- Resource overcommitments are rare or planned (for example, project overtime).
- Capacity planning is continuous.
- Success for the organization is measured by enterprise performance.
- Enterprise knowledge is managed and readily accessible.
- Successful program delivery becomes much more routine.

Depending on where you sit on the accountability continuum right now, this might seem like a list of impossible dreams. But we see companies who say they are experiencing these kinds of successes—very different kinds of organizations united in their accountability-based approach to management. HP, Coca-Cola Bottling Co. Consolidated, HSBC, Unilever, Best Buy, Bell South, Marlborough Stirling, MSC Software, T-Mobile, and the Georgia School Council Institute all display many of these ideal characteristics.

The way they've done it is to embrace transparency as a goal and to use the tools that we have discussed: portfolio management, processes, progress tracking, and knowledge management. All of these companies came to enjoy these benefits by implementing these steps in a similar manner. We've spent most of the book discussing the individual components of this system. This final chapter looks at the challenge from what we imagine might be your perspective: Where do we start?

In short; the answer is the following:

1. Do the culture thing.
2. Create a foundation.
3. Get a basic measurement.
4. Standardize your delivery model.
5. Measure and improve organizational capacity.
6. Partner with your customers.

1. Do the Culture Thing

People who run very effective knowledge organizations typically see nothing remarkable about the need for adult supervision. They cannot even describe their culture easily because an accountable culture is not particularly remarkable, outlandish, whimsical, or filled with unusual characters.

If your culture is not where you want it, don't worry that you'll have to spend 20 hours a week on it for months to "fix" it or spend all your time holding hands and giving soothing, encouraging pep talks. Have the conversations we discussed in Chapter 3, and make it clear from this day forward that things have changed and we're going to run this company in an accountable way. Lay down the basic rules and expectations. Then, be consistent in how you manage in light of those basic assumptions.

When Marlborough Stirling entered into a joint venture with a new company with the improbable name of Egg, it took great pains to make sure they broadcast the message that *things are different now*. Dave Phillips, the CFO, explains that they started it off with a big event, a joint venture party. They ordered a wedding cake. All 40 of Phillips's staff and all 200 of the Egg staff attended. Invitations were mailed out prior to the event. At the party, there was role playing (including a chorus of "I do's"), music, and general merriment. They sent pieces of the wedding cake, packaged in little plastic boxes, with an announcement, to the local papers, important clients, and other members of their target market. Do not confuse this with loopy team-building antics and other stuff that we have pooh-poohed in previous chapters. This was a milestone event; it signaled a new chapter for these employees.

The partners then followed it up with some very targeted activities designed to make sure everybody got the deal straight. They did a fresh set of appraisals for everybody. They also created an entirely new set of performance objectives. These were tied both to employees' roles, reinforcing hierarchy, as well as to customer satisfaction. They also changed the workspace for the Egg people. They stayed in the same building, but they moved desks around. This gave everyone a new vantage point, something new to look at. By remapping the workspace, they made it clear that the people were now part of a new organization. If you are consistent as a leader trying to reinforce an accountable culture, you'll find it will become self-policing. It is not, as Rhonda likes to remind people, rocket science. We are talking about basic, grown-up behavior. Expect it of your people, and they are likely to deliver it.

2. Create a Foundation

The next step is to take an initial assessment of your organization's work. Create a program catalog. This is your portfolio, version 1. There should be one line for each program your organization is working on. Identify the group or person responsible for delivering each program, the customer, the expected start and end dates, and the expected deliverable or benefit. Any work that is being done in the organization that cannot define any of these attributes should either be canceled or put on hold. This is the first phase in portfolio management: Define. It communicates priorities and provides a framework for accountability.

This is all about understanding what your organization is doing. This portfolio becomes your simple list of accepted programs. Make it clear: People should not be working on anything that is not on the list.

Simply writing down all of the programs that your organization is working on will enable you to progress to the second phase in portfolio management: Review. You should be able to easily identify redundant programs and analyze them as to whether they should be combined. Also, if any programs do not have a customer or sponsor, you will be identifying unneeded programs. These two activities typically result in some reduction in work for your organization.

Also during this step, you should work to get people to start collaborating. You'll really get into this in the fourth step, but collaboration has almost no cost and a big benefit. Find a collaboration tool. (By this we mean a program that facilitates collaboration. E-mail is a rudimentary collaboration tool. More advanced systems would include document sharing, discussion, and notification capabilities. Examples are products like *Lotus Notes*, or something more enterprise encompassing such as our *Niku 6* product.) And tell everyone to create a collaboration program, one for every program in your portfolio. Each collaboration program will be a shared area for your knowledge workers to work in. The program owner, the person responsible for delivering the program, should set this up. The benefits here should be a reduction in work, and, for the stars in your organization, more efficiency because of collaboration.

Meet with all of your direct reports once a week to get their progress and have them prepare a status report for these meetings.

3. Get a Basic Measurement

The next step is progress tracking. Process Queen that I am, I would have thought that processes should be next, but our customers tell us otherwise. The problem with process definition is that a quantitative metric first needs to be identified to help focus the process work that will be done in the next step.

This step provides that essential quantitative metric. Because you probably don't have consistent plans for all of your programs in your portfolio, this information will not be useful in updating your schedules, but it will help you understand how much effort remains for each program.

You'll need a little help here. You'll need some time-tracking software, also called a *time and attendance system*. Our product, *Niku 6*, includes such a capability for an entire enterprise. Other systems address specific industry segments. Figure out how much effort you saved getting rid of redundant and unnecessary programs in the previous step and reinvest some of that cost savings into a time tracking system and a really good program manager.

Program managers provide visibility in an organization. Program managers are responsible for defining process and providing an infrastructure to all program initiatives. Their charter typically includes combining common and repeatable processes, methodologies, and tools (software and templates) across an organization to:

- Clearly establish enterprise priorities to ensure alignment with corporate strategic initiatives
- Enable better and more consistent portfolio decisions (programs, projects, and operational workgroups)
- Optimize the deployment of enterprise resources across the portfolio
- Improve overall enterprise capacity planning
- Ensure consistent and repeatable results by setting standards and guidelines
- Make crucial enterprise knowledge accessible across the enterprise
- Develop and sustain experienced and knowledgeable project managers
- Lower operating costs and program and/or project startup costs by leveraging common processes and tools

Certainly a tall order. But in our experience, program managers can help do all these things. This is the infrastructure that can provide you with a sustained competitive advantage. Our rule of thumb is that program managers should be about 2 percent of your organization's resources.

Program managers typically work in a group called the *program office*. They report to the head of the organization. So, decide to either be the program office yourself, or hire someone with the skills. The program office's first task will be to select and implement a time tracking system. They will also need to train everyone in the organization in its use. They will be responsible for tracking compliance, and they will prepare the time reports for all the managers. Just to be clear, the program office—whether you're a CEO establishing an office to reflect 2 percent of your resources, or whether you're a project manager with a 25-person team about to assign "half" a person to this task—operates under your direction. It is implementing the things you want implemented.

Once you start getting time reports, you can then understand how much of your organization's efforts are being expended on which programs. On a weekly or monthly basis, you can determine if the importance of the program is matched by the scope of the effort expended. This corresponds to the third phase in portfolio management: Prioritize. This forces alignment and allows the analysis of tradeoffs. With progress tracking, you can verify that you are truly aligned. You can verify that you have truly killed those unnecessary programs, and you can verify that your organization is really working on the most important things in the right priority order. This will also probably give you an opportunity to analyze some tradeoffs.

This will probably be the first place where you can have an intelligent and even refreshingly optimistic conversation with customers. You can show your demand side how the supply side is doing. You can tell your customers, "Things have changed. And now you can see our new focus is on making you happy, not finding plausible excuses for why we are late or inadequate." Put all this together, and you now have a speedometer. You've just achieved visibility on your organization's efforts. Think of the possibilities. If you truly knew how much your organization was expending on any particular customer, you would be able to align your efforts more effectively with the programs that generate the greatest benefits. You would be able to spot trends, and you would begin to have the visibility to take action early and nip some problems in the bud.

Of course, most programs in your portfolio do not have a plan. To this point, you have not tracked progress so much as you have tracked effort. This gives you a good backward look at what your organization did. In order to determine how your organization will do in the future, you must go on to the next step.

4. Standardize the Delivery Methodology

Dear readers, as we come around the bend here, look to the left side of the boat and you will get another excellent view of the Dibachi shrine to process . . .

You get real-time visibility by standardizing your processes. This allows you to define and quantify progress. Process is important because if you standardize on a method, everyone can use it.

You are going to be working on processes in this step. You're going to start creating your business processes and your project management processes. You will use knowledge management to turn existing best practices into processes everyone can use.

All of your programs will soon have plans. With progress tracking, you'll begin implementing closed-loop project control. Your program office will be the workhorse here, helping create these processes and training the organization in using them.

As if you couldn't tell, this is Rhonda's favorite step.

If you began using the collaboration tools in step 2, you should have a number of documents that you can use as the basis for creating your business processes. Use these as your beginning business processes, and resist the urge to embellish. Only develop business processes for those activities that are using more than 15 percent of your organization's resources. Process is powerful, but it can also be a deep morass into which detail-oriented people are sucked, never to be heard from again. By minimizing the scope of your business process definition activity to include only frequently used activities, you can get a great set of documented business processes for a small amount of effort. You will begin to start capturing the vast amounts of explicit knowledge in your organization.

Who should do this work? You have two choices here. You can use your program managers to do this step. They should work with the best knowledge workers in your organization, the ones who have the information in the collaboration system. Or you can nominate a program manager from your program office to become a process guru. Some program offices split their work into two areas: program management and business processes. For large organizations, for consistency, a process group helps define and disseminate best practices. (If you are aiming for Six Sigma, this is a required step.) Based on our experience with customers, if an organization has a program office of more than 10 people, you need both organizations: a program office as well as a process group.

Next, create your project management processes. We have said that you can use any number of standards in this area, but we like the Project Management Institute's. Concentrate first on the planning, performing, and correcting phases. These will show your people how to work their programs. You can use your program managers to do this step, as well.

Review and approve these processes. After that, the process group and program managers train everyone in the organization on their use.

Take a look at your portfolio: For every program that is less than 75 percent complete and takes up more than 5 percent of the resources, make them go through the planning phase of the project management process. Each program owner should be able to deliver to you a plan, with steps, deliverables, a list of resources and their schedule commitments, a schedule, and a budget. Add all these to your collaboration system. The program owners should baseline the schedule and the budget. Update your portfolio with this new information, adding a budget column.

In this way, you will be improving the quality of your data by verifying these program plans. Don't worry about killing off any programs in this phase; simply concentrate on improving data quality.

Get people to start tracking progress against the new plans for all programs. Implement closed-loop project control. On a weekly basis have progress reports update project schedules. Also on a weekly basis, update your portfolio information with this data. This improves your visibility by allowing you to compare apples to apples. Everything should be scheduled using roughly the same rules, so you should start seeing some kind of information consistency.

Use your newfound visibility to communicate more information to your customers. Set up weekly meetings with customers. Routinely involve them in weekly updates, and make sure they are apprised of their programs' progress and consulted when problems erupt. You'll be getting consistent information, which will make it easier for you to communicate to your customers. It is quantitative as well, and your customers will begin to value and trust this information.

Now you know what to work on, you know what your people are working on, you know that they are starting to do it more efficiently, you know where they are in their delivery, and they are adding value by delivering information more quickly to your customers. But what you don't know is how your organization is doing from an efficiency standpoint.

5. Measure and Improve Organizational Capacity

You've started to get an understanding of what your organization is doing. But is it fast? Is it slow? How many people with what skill sets should work on every program? What allocation percentage should be applied to those people? What is the estimated future program demand? This step allows you to level resources across the demand load to determine what can be delivered. If you understand your organizational capacity, you can actually start getting better at your on-time deliveries. Soon you'll stop arguing that the metrics FedEx might use to track package delivery don't apply to you. You'll embrace the idea that knowledge work can be more efficient and predictable.

You should also be getting some cost numbers now. Since you know how much effort is expended in each program, figure out how much every program costs by multiplying your standard corporate overhead rate by your people's salaries for the duration of the program. Use this cost information when adding the last two phases to your project management processes: initiating and closing.

The closing phase for the project management process should give you enough information for you to figure out a couple of things:

- Where are your bottlenecks?
- Where are there more opportunities for collaboration?

By taking a look at your organization's results on a program-by-program basis, you can identify bottlenecks. Where are you consistently falling down? Where does your organization consistently overshoot its estimates? It's all about finding inefficiencies and fixing them. You now have the data to do it. Use the information in your knowledge store to find opportunities for process improvement. You have it all there. As you close programs, when mistakes are fresh in everyone's mind, start updating your business processes to improve them so that these mistakes never occur again. The same people who close out a program should be the ones who improve the process. Or, if you've decided to invest in a full-scale business process group, they can help.

You could also figure this out using project management resource maps. Lay out all steps of the process and cross-reference these with the skills required to complete each step. Adding resource loading and timelines can show you where your bottlenecks are. You are trying to find the root causes of delivery and nondelivery. You are trying to determine the critical factors for your organization's success.

You know how much each of your people can do since you have the data. Challenge them to improve it. Can they reduce their time to put out a press release by 10 percent?

If you ask that question early in this overhaul, your public relations staff will instinctively tell you that that is a ridiculous sort of goal. Every press release is unique, triggered by often unpredictable circumstances, requiring different sorts of approvals, and linked to outside forces. Agreed. But ask them: What is the typical path of a press release? Now, where are the bottlenecks? For example, do you typically wait to schedule a "reading" by the CEO or other approver until the release is written? Does that person's dissatisfaction then result in a total rewrite? Would a more direction-packed meeting with that person prior to the document being written reduce the later need for rewrites? Life is not a controlled experiment. You can't go back and re-experience the event and try something different. But you can consider options that attack known bottlenecks, and you can work them until the bottlenecks widen.

Marlborough Stirling focused a lot on this step when it merged with Egg. They looked at all of the new business that had recently been defined. They mapped out a proper workflow for each process to identify which roles needed to perform which steps. Then, using the information from time tracking, they figured out which steps were taking the longest. They concentrated on reducing the amount of time it took to complete the steps. They created scoreboards, and they gave everyone targets. They started articulating their goals and measuring their results. It was simply a process improvement activity. The program office, with its experience in working with processes, helped improve the business processes of the joint venture.

Goals were given to teams, not just the program owners. With a common goal, everybody became more motivated. It was the same people who were doing the same things, but they began doing them better.

When you've worked through the overhang of existing work, add the initiating phase of your project management process. From now on, all new initiatives need to go through this phase. First, take the programs in your portfolio and let them go through an initiating phase. (Do this only for the high value-added programs, those that are less than 75 percent completed and those that take up more than 5 percent of your organization's resources.) In order to reapprove all of the programs in your portfolio, you can either do this review yourself or you can create a strategy group. The strategy group is used effectively in some organizations. It acts as a funnel, taking all new opportunities and weeding out the old and the weak. These people are horizon scanners; they look for new opportunities and are experts at analyzing them. Their job is to verify that new opportunities are analyzed and the portfolio is balanced.

Regardless of whether you do this yourself or have a strategy group to do this for you, you have progressed to the fifth phase of portfolio management: Balance. You can begin to value a particular division's contributions to the company. You can also make intelligent business decisions based on the costs and benefits of the programs in your portfolio. You need to do this in conjunction with your program sponsors, or your customers. You need an excellent understanding of the true benefits of each of these programs. That's why, as we mentioned earlier, Maynard Webb makes internal customers present and justify a business case before he'll commit IT resources. This is another step toward the eventual goal of a true partnership with your customers.

After taking a look at all important existing programs, and forcing them to go through the initiation phase, you're doing world-class opportunity management. You are asking that all programs be analyzed as opportunities. This will result in some tough decisions, but you will have the quantitative data to make your point. You'll be able to show your customers, your executives, and your people that the portfolio as it stands delivers the greatest value to your organization. Or you'll make the case that certain management bottlenecks exist that make it impossible to maximize productivity.

6. Partner with Your Customers

The final, but also never-ending sixth step is partnering with customers. This is a process, a journey! New opportunities come in and are analyzed by your strategy group. Then the good ones go down the chute. Tradeoffs are made between new opportunities and existing programs based on cost and benefit information. Programs are managed using best-practices project management processes. Your business processes are well-known. People share knowledge routinely. Explicit knowledge is constantly encoded to improve your processes. Tacit knowledge is shared routinely using collaboration.

Your program owners have steadily shifted from being mostly internally focused to being externally focused. As the organization becomes more and more capable of facing the challenges of everyday life, your program owners concentrate on managing external relationships. They get closer and closer to their customers, and they start understanding their customers' needs more clearly than ever before. They give their customers greater visibility and educate them about processes. Customers are approached as partners rather than adversaries. Customers are willingly engaged and actively help with prioritization, business case definition, and problem solving. Your program owners want to know if they deliver something to the customer, what will the customer be able to do? They always know the customer's critical issues.

Here, your organization is concentrating more on the outcomes of your program work. No longer are the inputs the most important thing. It is not enough simply to bring a program to completion on budget and on schedule. Rather, the most important thing is to actually be able to deliver the business value. Process inputs and outcomes are defined, managed, and measured. Customers are added to the knowledge management process loop. They share in the definition of explicit knowledge, and they share in the transfer of tacit knowledge. You have given them quantitative information on progress and have engaged them throughout all program progress.

You constantly improve your business processes with their help. Customer feedback allows you to correctly focus on continuously improving the methodologies you have. Instead of change for change's sake, you will change something only if doing so delivers greater value to your customer.

Continuous process improvement will turn your static organization into a learning organization. You will begin to foster a culture of change and innovation. You will find that mistakes are confronted routinely and corrected. Your organization is reengineered. Your visibility is good.

Of course, you wouldn't be where you are without your knowledge workers. They're the ones who fuel your organization. They are your worker bees, they are your program managers, they are your business process experts, and they are your strategy group. They'll know what to do because they have the deal straight, they respect hierarchy, and they're totally customer focused. They understand priorities, process, and progress. And best of all, they are actively engaged in sharing their knowledge. It is as easy to them as breathing.

Checklists and Templates

S EE ALSO WWW.NIKU.COM for downloadable versions of these and other checklists and templates.

General Checklists and Templates

Weekly Status Report Template

Weekly Status Report			
Programs	Progress	Plans	Problems

Candidate Interview Assessment Checklist

- Does the candidate demonstrate a mature and accountable attitude toward work? Does he or she understand the basic value proposition of the workplace and articulate the value he or she brings?
- Can the candidate articulate previous job responsibilities?
- Can the candidate clearly articulate a link between the previous employer's strategic goals and his or her own responsibilities?
- Does the candidate appear to respect hierarchy in general? Does the candidate seem to respect your opinion?
- Does the candidate exhibit any toxic knowledge worker behaviors, such as harboring resentments, ridiculing coworkers or managers, or showing disrespect for process and accountability? If the worker is negative about past experiences, are the complaints concrete or are they indicative of an antiaccountability mindset?
- Has the individual considered what resources he or she needs to be successful, including time, training, and other people?
- Does the candidate demonstrate an understanding and sensitivity to customers? Can he or she identify and articulate a clear relationship to customers in past positions? Does the candidate refer to customers in a negative way?

Employee Performance Review Checklist

- Do you know why you are here? What is it that I am paying you to do?
- What are your job responsibilities?
- Do you understand the company's strategic initiatives and direction?
- How do you feel about the priorities that have been articulated to you? Do you agree with those priorities? How do you intend to carry them out? Are you clear on my authority to communicate these priorities?
- Do I listen to you? Do you feel that I solicit your opinion?
- Do you have what you need to be successful?
- Who is your customer? What are his or her needs? What are you doing to fill those needs? How is whatever it is you're doing taking into account customer needs?

- Do you understand that the company owns your work products?
- What can I do to make you more successful?
- What are the key mistakes we seem to make over and over again, and can you suggest some way we can avoid making them?
- How can you perform your job 10 percent more efficiently?
- Do you feel that the company's demands on your time are reasonable? Do you understand why extraordinary demands are sometimes made?

Portfolio Management Templates

Step I. Template for Defining the Portfolio

Program	Sponsor or Customer	Time Frame	Program Owner

Step 2. Template for Reviewing the Portfolio

Program	Sponsor or Customer	Start Date	Expected End Date	Number of Resources Assigned	Program Owner

Step 3. Template for Measuring the Value of and Prioritizing the Portfolio

Program	Sponsor or Customer	Start Date	Expected End Date	Number of Resources Assigned	Benefit	Cost	Value	Program Owner
							Sort all programs in this column	
Total					*Total benefit of portfolio*	*Total cost of portfolio*	*Total value of portfolio*	

Step 4. Template for Categorizing the Work in the Portfolio

Management Objective or Strategic Initiative	Program	Sponsor or Customer	Start Date	Expected End Date	Number of Resources Assigned	Benefit	Cost	Value	Program Owner
Sort by the objective/ strategic initiative.	Show all programs that belong to that objective or initiative.								
Total						*Total benefit of portfolio*	*Total cost of portfolio*	*Total value of portfolio*	

Step 5. Template for Balancing the Portfolio

Management Objective or Strategic Initiative	Program	Sponsor or Customer	Start Date	Expected End Date	Number of Resources Assigned	Benefit	Cost	Value	Program Owner
Total for objective or initiative					*Total number of resources for all programs in that category*	*Total benefit for all programs in that category*	*Total cost for all programs in that category*	*Total value for all programs in that category*	
Grand Total						*Total benefit of portfolio*	*Total cost of portfolio*	*Total value of portfolio*	

Step 6. Template for Managing the Portfolio

Management Objective or Strategic Initiative	Program	Sponsor or Customer	Start Date	Expected End Date	Number of Resources Assigned	Benefit	Cost	Value	Program Owner
Total for objective or initiative					*Total number of resources for all programs in that category*	*Total benefit for all programs in that category*	*Total cost for all programs in that category*	*Total value for all programs in that category*	
Grand Total						*Total benefit of portfolio*	*Total cost of portfolio < or = total budget for the organization*	*Total value of portfolio*	

Project Management Templates and Checklists

Phase I. Initiation Templates for an Internal Opportunity

General Information	
Name of opportunity	
Customer or sponsor name	
Brief description of the recommended solution	
Solution to be delivered in what time frame?	
Brief history of the situation or problem, including attempts to solve	
Business sponsors?	
Which strategic initiatives does this support?	
How will this affect customers?	
How will this affect our business?	
How will this affect our partners?	
Is this dependent on other programs that are not yet completed? What is the probability that these other programs will be completed in the expected time frame?	
Any special or extraordinary risks?	

Benefits over an X-Year Period

Hard Savings over an X-Year Period			
	Value (Net Present Value)	Certainty or Risk	Weighted Value (Value × Certainty)
Reduced headcount			
Reduced capital expenses			
Reduced overhead			
Reduced facilities charges			
Reduced IT charges			
Reduced contractor charges			
Other hard savings			
Total hard savings			*Total hard savings*
Soft Savings over an X-Year Period			
Increased efficiency			
Decreased errors			
Decreased legal fees			
Increased transaction processing speed			
Total soft savings			*Total soft savings*
Total savings			*Total savings (hard + soft)*

Costs over an X-Year period			
	Value (Net Present Value)	Certainty or Risk	Weighted Value (Value × Certainty)
People			
Capital expenses (please list)			
Leases			
Consultants and/or contractors			
Other operating expenses			
Total costs			*Total costs*
Total value of opportunity = total savings – total costs			

Phase I. Initiation Templates for an External Opportunity

General Information	
Name of opportunity	
Customer	
Brief description of the opportunity	
Time frame for delivery	
Time frame for receiving the benefit	
Business sponsors?	
Which strategic initiatives does this support?	
How will this affect other customers?	
How will this affect our business?	
How will this affect our partners?	
Any special or extraordinary risks?	

Revenues over an X-Year Period

Hard Revenues over an X-Year Period			
	Value (Net Present Value)	Certainty or Risk	Weighted Value (Value × Certainty)
Increased sales in existing markets			
Increased sales in new markets (please list)			
Increased distribution channels			
Increased margins			
Increased size of sales			
Reduced customer returns			
Other hard revenues			
Total hard revenues			*Total hard revenues*
Soft Revenues over an X-Year Period			
Increased number of potential customers			
Increased likelihood to buy			
Increased customer satisfaction			
Increased number of repeat customers			
Total soft revenues			*Total soft revenues*
Total revenues			*Total revenues (hard + soft)*

Costs over an X-Year period			
	Value (Net Present Value)	Certainty or Risk	Weighted Value (Value × Certainty)
People			
Capital expenses (please list)			
Leases			
Consultants and/or contractors			
Other operating expenses			
Total costs			*Total costs*
Total value of opportunity = total revenues – total costs			

Phase 2. Planning Templates

Program Plan Template	
Program name	
Sponsor or customer	
Expected start date	
Actual start date	
Expected end date	
Actual end date	
Program owner	
Program manager	
Expected program benefits	
Actual program benefits	
Expected program costs	
Actual program costs	
Expected program value	
Actual program value	
Business process to be followed, (include any special steps or changes)	
Any special risks for this program?	
Any special issues for this program?	
Does this program depend on any other program? What would the effects be on this program if the dependant program were to have problems?	

Program Steps Template

Step Number	Step Name or Description	Resources, Roles or Skills Required, Type and Number	Start Date		End Date		Deliverables	Other Costs, Including Contractors, Materials, etc.	Step Completion Verified By?
			Expected	Forecast or actual	Expected	Forecast or actual			

Phase 2. Planning Checklist

- Program charter has been completed.
- Program charter has been communicated to all team members.
- Program risks have been discussed with all team members.
- All team members understand their responsibilities.
- The program plan was developed with the participation of the team members.
- The program plan has been completed.
- All team members understand the program plan.
- The customer understands the program plan.
- Suppliers understand the program plan.
- Steps in the program plan are defined, along with their costs, resources, deliverables, and verification criteria.
- Required resources have been committed.
- Each step has a time estimate.
- Each step has a cost estimate.
- Allowances have been made for holidays, sick days, vacations, and so on.
- The plan contains enough collaboration steps to ensure quality work.
- The budget has been approved.
- The schedule has been approved.
- Completed programs, similar to this, which were successful, have been reviewed, and have helped in the development of this program plan.

Phases 3 and 4. Checklist for Program Manager's Responsibilities

- Works with program team to identify project goal or charter
- Works with program team to define program plan
- Communicates plan to his or her manager as well as to the team
- Determines resource requirements and seeks commitment
- Calculates overall schedule, overall budget, and total program value
- Helps select team members
- Defines each team member's responsibilities
- Defines clear roles and responsibilities for each team member
- Periodically reviews program status

- Reviews all deliverables
- Reviews and approves all expenditures
- Manages to a budget
- Manages to a schedule
- Periodically reviews status, progress, and variances with his or her manager
- Holds periodic program meetings
- Communicates progress, changes, and issues to team members
- Assesses the quality of work
- Leads team in the program
- Recognizes team and individual successes, as well as failures
- Delegates tasks as appropriate
- Spots problems in real time
- Changes status to trouble program, if necessary
- Works with all team members to improve plan for a trouble program
- Openly collaborates with all team members to improve program plan
- Works with customer, assumes overall responsibility for program
- Communicates plan, status, progress, changes, and issues to customer
- Verifies customer approval on each step
- Openly collaborates with customer to improve plan
- Ties the program's success to the success of the company
- Communicates benefits in terms of business value
- Aligns program's success with corporate strategic initiatives

Phase 5. Template for Project Closing

Capturing Lessons Learned for Business Processes			
What Was Important?	**How Was It Captured?**	**What Does It Represent?**	**How Will It Be Handled?**
What you did	A deliverable	An interesting twist	Keep it in context, with the other deliverables for that program, in a historical archive for future reference.
		New best practice	Modify the template for the deliverable.
			Add this as a great example of a great deliverable.
The way you did it	A process step	An interesting twist	Keep it in context, as a record of the process taken for that program, in a historical archive for future reference.
		New best practice	Modify the process to include this new step.
			Add it as a guideline to the process.

Checklist for Closing a Project

- Did we achieve our goals? Did we perform on our promises?
- How can we verify this? Whom did we ask? (The correct answer is: The customer.)
- Were the cost and effort variances within 10 percent of the initial projections? Were they acceptable?
- If not, what were the reasons for the cost or effort overruns?
- Was the project charter properly and completely defined?
- Was the program owner in charge? Or did team members question his or her authority? What can be done to assert this hierarchy in the future?
- Were there resource scheduling problems? Were key resources overscheduled? Not available? Not experienced enough? How can we prevent such problems in the future?
- Were key resources ever pulled off the program to work on something else? What can we do to prevent this from happening in the future?
- Was there consistent communication with the customer? Was the customer surprised at any step? Did we not communicate with the customer when we should have?
- Did we spend too much? Was excessive spending the result of other problems? What was the root cause of the overspend?
- Did we deliver the full scope of the solution? If not, how can we better estimate the amount of effort it will take to deliver a solution with this scope?
- Was the process followed? Were any steps skipped or performed differently? Was anything added? Did these changes make the solution better or worse?
- Were effort estimates realistic? Did we plan enough time for all steps? Which steps were problems? Why did they take too long? Was the estimate too short, or did problems occur that complicated the activity?
- Did the team work as a team?

Endnotes

Introduction

[1]Wendy Zellner and Stephanie Anderson Forest in Dallas, with Emily Thornton, Peter Coy, Heather Timmons, and David Henry in New York, and bureau reports, "The Fall of Enron," *Business Week*, December 17, 2001, p. 30.

[2]U.S. Bureau of the Census, "Labor Force, Employment, and Earnings: No. 593. Employed Civilians by Occupation, Sex, Race, and Hispanic Origin: 1983 and 2000," *Statistical Abstract of the United States*, 2001, Washington, D.C., 2001.

[3]U.S. Department of Labor, Bureau of Labor Statistics, *International Comparisons of Labor Productivity and Unit Labor Costs in Manufacturing, 2000*, Washington, D.C., April 2002.

Chapter I

[1]"Chuck" is not the manager's real name, but his predicament as we've described it actually occurred to a real manager in a large financial services company.

[2]U.S. Bureau of the Census, "Labor Force, Employment, and Earnings: No. 593. Employed Civilians by Occupation, Sex, Race, and Hispanic Origin: 1983 and 2000," *Statistical Abstract of the United States, 2001*, Washington, D.C., 2001. We use Fritz Machlup's definition of *knowledge workers* based on occupational structure. From *The Production and Distribution of Knowledge in the United States*, Princeton University Press, Princeton, NJ, 1962. Machlup defined *white collar worker* as a person who produces knowledge. Knowledge-producing occupations include the managerial and professional specialities and the technical, sales, and administrative support occupations.

[3]For services productivity, see Jack Triplett and Barry Bosworth, "Productivity in the Services Sector," *Brookings Economic Papers*, January 2000. The authors of this paper, which was prepared for the American Economic Association Session on Productivity in Services, January 9, 2000, suggest that there was actually a 2 percentage point slowdown in the services sector from 1973 to 1996. For detailed analysis of productivity in the manufacturing sector, see U.S. Bureau of Labor Statistics, *International Comparisons of Labor Productivity and Unit Labor Costs in Manufacturing, 2000*, Washington, D.C., April 2002. Output per hour for manufacturing increased from 3.3 to 5.5 percent in the years 1990 to 1999.

[4]Peter F. Drucker, "Knowledge Worker Productivity, The Biggest Challenge," *California Management Review*, The Regents of the University of California, vol. 41, no. 2, winter 1999.

[5]U.S. Department of Labor, Bureau of Labor Statistics, "Labor Force Projections to 2010: Steady Growth and Changing Composition," *Monthly Labor Review*, November 2001.

Chapter 2

[1]Robert Frank and Deborah Solomon, "Adelphia Paid Founding Family Many Millions," *Wall Street Journal*, May 28, 2002, p. A6.

Chapter 3

[1]Tim Sanders, *Love Is the Killer App: How to Win Business and Influence Friends*, Crown Publishers, New York, 2002.

Chapter 5

[1]Robert S. Kaplan and David P. Norton, *The Balanced Scorecard*, Harvard Business School Press, Boston, 1995.

Chapter 6

[1] For these and others, see Harold Kerzer, *Project Management: A Systems Approach to Planning, Scheduling, and Controlling*, 7th ed., Wiley, New York, 2000. Anything you ever wanted to know about project management.

[2]The details of EVA are beyond the scope of this book, but an excellent description of it can be found in James P. Lewis, *Project Manager's Desk Reference*, 2nd ed., McGraw-Hill, Boston, 2000.

Chapter 7

[1]William Thomson, 1st Baron Kelvin of Largs (1824–1907), a British mathematician and physicist. In 1848 proposed the absolute, or Kelvin, temperature scale.

[2]Elton Mayo, *The Human Problems of an Industrial Civilization*, MacMillan, New York, 1933.

Bibliography

Berinto, Scott. "Do the Math." *CIO Magazine*, October 1, 2001. http://www.cio.com/archive/100101/math.html, accessed June 14, 2002.

Brooking, Annie. *Corporate Memory: Strategies for Knowledge Management.* London: International Thomson Business Press, 1999.

————. *Intellectual Capital: Core Asset for the Third Millennium.* London: International Thomson Business Press, 1996.

Brooks, Frederick P., Jr. *The Mythical Man-Month: Essays on Software Engineering.* Reading, Mass.: Addison-Wesley, 1982.

Cortada, James W., ed. *Rise of the Knowledge Worker.* Boston: Butterworth-Heinemann, 1998.

Crosby, Philip B. *Quality Is Free: The Art of Making Quality Certain.* New York: McGraw-Hill, 1979; New York: Mentor Books, 1992.

————. *Quality without Tears: The Art of Hassle-Free Management.* New York: McGraw-Hill, 1984. Reprint, New York: Penguin Group, Plume, 1985.

Davenport, Thomas H., and Laurence Prusak. *Working Knowledge: How Organizations Manage What They Know.* Boston: Harvard Business School Press, 1998.

Drucker, Peter F. "Knowledge Worker Productivity: The Biggest Challenge." *California Management Review*, The Regents of the University of California, vol. 41, no. 2, winter 1999.

Edvinsson, Leif, and Michael S. Malone. *Intellectual Capital: Realizing Your Company's True Value by Finding Its Hidden Brainpower.* New York: HarperBusiness, 1997.

Ewert, David C. *Finance for Project Managers.* Lake Forest, Ill.: Lake Forest Graduate School of Management, 2001.

Frank, Robert, and Deborah Solomon. "Adelphia Paid Founding Family Many Millions." *Wall Street Journal*, May 28, 2002, p. A6.

Fitz-enz, Jac. *The ROI of Human Capital: Measuring the Economic Value of Employee Performance.* New York: Amacom, 2000.

Goldsmith, Marshall, Laurence Lyons, Alyssa Freas, and Robert Witherspoon, eds. *Coaching for Leadership: How the World's Greatest Coaches Help Leaders Learn.* San Francisco: Jossey-Bass/Pfeiffer, 2000.

Hansen, Morten T., Nitin Nohria, and Thomas Tierney. "What's Your Strategy for Managing Knowledge?" *Harvard Business Review*, March-April 1999, pp. 106–116.

Heskett, James L., W. Earl Sasser, Jr., and Leonard A. Schlesinger. *The Service Profit Chain: How Leading Companies Link Profit and Growth to Loyalty, Satisfaction, and Value.* New York: Free Press, 1997.

Kaplan, Robert S., and David P. Norton. "The Balanced Scorecard—Measures That Drive Performance." *Harvard Business Review*, January–February 1992, pp. 71–79.

————, and David P. Norton. *The Balanced Scorecard: Translating Strategy into Action.* Boston: Harvard Business School Press, 1996.

————, and David P. Norton. *The Strategy-Focused Organization: How Balanced Scorecard Companies Thrive in the New Business Environment.* Boston: Harvard Business School Press, 2001.

Kerzner, Harold. *Project Management: A Systems Approach to Planning, Scheduling, and Controlling,* 7th ed. New York: Wiley, 2000.

Kim, W. Chan, and Renée Mauborgne. "Fair Process: Managing in the Knowledge Economy." *Harvard Business Review,* July–August 1997.

Kouzes, James M., and Barry Z. Posner. *Encouraging the Heart: A Leader's Guide to Rewarding and Recognizing Others.* San Francisco: Jossey-Bass, 1999.

Kramer, R. M., and T. R. Tyler, eds. *Trust in Organizations: Frontiers of Theory and Research.* Thousand Oaks, Calif.: Sage, 1996.

Labovitz, George, and Victor Rosansky. *The Power of Alignment: How Great Companies Stay Centered and Accomplish Extraordinary Things.* New York: Wiley, 1997.

Lewis, James P. *The Project Manager's Desk Reference,* 2nd ed. Boston: McGraw-Hill, 2000.

Mayo, Elton. *The Human Problems of an Industrial Civilization.* New York: MacMillan, 1933.

McGrath, Michael E. *Setting the PACE in Product Development: A Guide to Product and Cycle-time Excellence.* Boston: Butterworth-Heinemann, 1996.

Pfeffer, Jeffrey, and Robert I. Sutton. *The Knowing-Doing Gap: How Smart Companies Turn Knowledge into Action.* Boston: Harvard Business School Press, 2000.

Project Management Institute (PMI). *A Guide to the Project Management Book of Knowledge (PMBOK), 2000 edition.* Newtown Square, Penn.: Project Management Institute, 2000.

Quinn, James Brian, Jordan J. Baruch, and Karen Anne Zien. *Innovation Explosion: Using Intellect and Software to Revolutionize Growth Strategies.* New York: Free Press, 1997.

Rummler, Geary A., and Alan P. Brache. *Improving Performance: How to Manage the White Space on the Organization Chart,* 2nd ed. San Francisco: Jossey-Bass, 1995.

Schreiber, Guus, Hans Akkermans, Anjo Anjewierden, Robert de Hoog, Nigel Shadbolt, Walter Van de Velde, and Bob Wielinga. *Knowledge Engineering and Management: The CommonKADS Methodology.* Cambridge, Mass: Bradford Books, 2000.

Sharpe, Paul, and Tom Keelin. "How SmithKline Beecham Makes Better Resource-Allocation Decisions." *Harvard Business Review,* March–April 1998.

Stewart, Thomas A. *Intellectual Capital: The New Wealth of Organizations.* New York: Doubleday, 1997.

Triplett, Jack, and Barry Bosworth. "Productivity in the Services Sector." *Brookings Economic Papers,* January 2000. Prepared for the American Economic Association Session on Productivity in Services, Boston, Massachusetts, January 9, 2000.

U.S. Bureau of the Census. "Labor Force, Employment, and Earnings: No. 593. Employed Civilians by Occupation, Sex, Race, and Hispanic Origin: 1983 and 2000." *Statistical Abstract of the United States: 2001.* Washington, D.C.: Government Printing Office.

U.S. Department of Labor, Bureau of Labor Statistics. *International Comparisons of Labor Productivity and Unit Labor Costs in Manufacturing, 2000.* Washington, D.C., April 2002. ftp://ftp.bls.gov/pub/special.requests/ForeignLabor/internatshort.txt, accessed June 14, 2002.

————. "Labor Force Projections to 2010: Steady Growth and Changing Composition. *Monthly Labor Review,* November 2001.

Wight, Oliver. *The Oliver Wight ABCD Checklist for Operational Excellence,* 4th ed. Essex Junction, Vt.: Oliver Wight Publications, 1993.

Index

Accenture, 104, 142–144
Accountability:
  corporate culture and, 62, 63
  for time, 19, 21–22, 123–124, 132–134, 192–194
Accountability Management System, 15–16, 21, 27–39
  basic deal in, 28–29, 38, 41–42, 45–47
  customer focus in, 31–33, 38, 41, 48–50, 196, 199–200
  hierarchy in, 29–31, 38, 41, 47–48, 58
  priorities in, 30–31, 33–34, 38, 64, 69, 70, 72, 75–94
  process in, 34–35, 38, 70–71, 95–122, 196–199
  progress tracking in, 35, 39, 123–144
  transparency and, 5
  working smart in, 30, 36, 39
Actual cost of work performed (ACWP), 110
Adams, Scott, 78
Adelphia Communications, Inc., 34–35
Adult supervision, 48
  corporate culture and, 190–191
  need for, 180
  transparency and, 5, 63, 72, 190–191
Alignment reports, 139
Ambition, of knowledge workers, 17–18, 23–24
American Productivity and Quality Center (APQC), 102
Analysis paralysis problem, 91
Andreessen, Marc, 17
Arthur Young, 12, 148, 150–151
Ash, Terry, 109, 125–126
Automation of tasks, 22–23, 162

Balanced scorecard approach, 85
Baseline plan:
  accurate data for, 127–128
  in progress tracking, 126–128
Basic deal:
  described, 28–29, 38
  determining employee understanding of, 45–47
  importance of, 41–42
Bear Stearns, 79–81, 158, 190
Bell South, 190
Berquist, Tom, 148–149
Best Buy, 190
Best practices, 70–71, 72, 116, 199
Big internal customer problem, 32–33, 49
Big-picture understanding, 18–19
British Telecommunications, 90
BT Exact, 90
Budget variances, 110, 111–113, 138–139, 144
Budgeted cost of work scheduled (BCWS), 110
Budgeting process, 89
Business process, 115–120
  defined, 100–101
  implementing, 120
  knowledge management and, 161
  nature of, 115–117
  priorities in, 117–120
  project management process versus, 101
  simplicity in, 120–122
  standardizing, 195

Closed-loop project control, 109, 125–126, 138–139, 195, 196
Closing phase, in project management, 113–115, 197

Coca-Cola Bottling Company Consolidated, 71–73, 113, 135–137, 190
Coleman, Patrick, 173
Collaboration:
  knowledge management and, 149–150, 156–159
  portfolio management and, 192, 196
Compaq, 43
Competitor information, 20, 178, 180–181
Constrained growth, 178
Continuous-improvement approach, 114–115, 200
Contribution margin, 118
Corporate culture:
  accountability and, 62, 63
  archetypes of knowledge workers, 50–55
  basic deal and, 45–47
  customer focus and, 48–50
  of Diba, 172–175, 187
  forced fun in, 56–58
  hierarchy in, 29–31, 38, 41, 47–48, 58
  knowledge management and, 149
  life outside work and, 24–25, 58–60
  ownership issues in, 56
  transparency and, 190–191
  visibility and, 61–64
Correcting phase, in project management, 111–113
Credibility, 43–44
Customer focus:
  big internal customer problem, 32–33, 49
  described, 31–33, 38
  determining employee understanding of, 48–50
  importance of, 41, 196
  partnering with customers, 199–200
Customer goals, 85
Customer relationship management (CRM), 3

"Dead men walking," 31, 169
Decimalization Project, 7–9, 11–12, 13–14
Dell, Michael, 17
Diba, 14, 165–188
  competitor information and, 178, 180–181
  corporate culture of, 172–175, 187
  development team of, 175–177
  difficulties of, 184–188
  family support for, 167, 168–169
  financing of, 169–170, 187–188
  forecasting growth of, 185
  growing pains of, 178–180
  infrastructure and, 170–171
  initial stages, 166–168
  nature of business, 165–166
  new building for, 186–187
  partnerships of, 175, 177–178, 179–180, 181, 184, 187
  press coverage of, 181–182

Diba (*Cont.*):
  product development and, 171–172
  sale to Sun Microsystems, 165, 172, 188
  trademark search and, 184–185
  typical week at, 182–184
Dilbert (cartoon), 78
Dishonesty, 62
Do-over tasks, 132
Drucker, Peter, 13
Deutsche Telekom, 66–67
Dumptruck reports, 66–67

E-mail:
  ownership of, 56
  teamwork and, 149–150, 192
Earned value analysis (EVA), 110
eBay, 36–38
Ebrahimi, Fred, 185
Egg, 191, 198
Elliott, John, 79–81, 158
Ellison, Larry, 17, 18, 43
Emotional insight, 17
Employees (*see* Knowledge workers)
Enron, 1, 2
Enterprise resource planning (ERP), 3
Enterprise software, 3, 154–155, 177, 192–194
Equity in company, 19–20
Estimate to complete (ETC), 129, 143
Excite, 2
Explicit knowledge:
  nature of, 152–155
  storing and updating, 159, 199

Feedback, in portfolio balancing, 88–89
Financial goals, 85
Flying-by-the-seat-of-your-pants project control, 125
Fonzarelli Factor, 43–44
Forty-hour workweek, 141–142
Foundation, importance of, 170–171

Gantt charts, 109–110, 125
Gates, Bill, 17, 18
General Electric, 12, 54, 168
Georgia School Council Institute, 190
"Get-it" culture, 1–2, 12, 14–15
Gillach, Joe, 171, 173, 183
Go-for-broke approach to growth, 178–179
Going-through-the-motions scenario, 142–144
Goto, Arnold, 18
Growth:
  approaches to, 178–180
  goals for, 85
  problems in forecasting, 185

Hard benefits/savings, 82–83
Hawthorne effect, 130–131, 134

Hewlett, Bill, 43
Hewlett-Packard, 43, 125–126, 168, 181, 190
Hierarchy:
  checks and balances on, 58
  described, 29–31, 38
  determining employee understanding of, 47–48
  importance of, 41
Hire-the-best-and-let-'em-rip mentality, 14
HSBC, 190

I Dream of Jeannie management, 102–103
Information:
  competitor, 20, 178, 180–181
  withholding key, 62
Initiation phase, of project management, 102–105, 126, 198–199
Inputs, confusing with outcomes, 67–69
Internal business process goals, 85
Internet Age, 2
Intracompany transfers, 49
Intranets, 152

Jewell, Fred, 104

Kaplan, Robert S., 85
Kelvin, Lord, 123
Knight, Licia, 142–144
Knowing-Doing Gap, The (Pfeffer), 21
Knowledge brokers, 162
Knowledge management, 69, 71, 145–163
  advanced approach to, 159–163
  collaboration in, 149–150, 156–159
  enterprise software for, 3, 154–155, 177, 192–194
  explicit knowledge and, 152–155, 159, 199
  historical approaches to, 147–149
  improving, 149–152
  knowledge store in, 159–163
  smart teamwork in, 149–150, 156–159
  tacit knowledge and, 155–158, 160–161, 199
  taxonomies in, 148, 153–154
Knowledge workers:
  archetypes of, 50–55
  characteristics of, 16–20
  could-go-either-way types, 53–54
  fixable types, 51–52
  impact of, 10
  motivation of (*see* Motivation)
  myths concerning, 20–25
  nature of, 10
  overworked, 141–142
  productivity of, 3–4, 10–11, 13, 15
  shape-up-or-ship-out types, 52–53
  toxic, 21, 35, 63

Knowledge workplace:
  management challenges in, 12–16
  myths concerning, 20–25
  nature of, 9–12
Kosmo, 68

Learning and growth goals, 85
Life outside work, 24–25, 58–60
Lloyd, Andy, 173
Lotus Notes, 150, 192

Management by getting out of the way, 3, 20–21
Management drive-by shooting, 8, 12–13, 132
Marathon working sessions, 24, 59
Marlborough Stirling, 48, 190, 191, 198
Mayo, Elton, 130–131
Mentor syndrome, 28–29, 47
Micromanagement, 14
Moore, Mark, 132, 171, 175–176, 177
Motivation, 41–60
  archetypes of knowledge workers, 50–55
  basic deal and, 45–47
  credibility of manager and, 43–44
  customer focus in, 48–50
  financial, 19–20, 44–45
  forced fun in, 56–58
  hierarchy and, 47–48, 58
  through recognition, 23–24, 44–45
Motorola, Inc., 114–115
MSC Software, 190
Myland, Jo, 19

New Economy, 1–2, 20, 34
Niku, 64, 97–98, 118, 132, 176–177, 182
Niku 6, 154–155, 177, 192–194
Nintendo generation, 16–17
Norton, David P., 85

Opportunity analysis, 90–93, 102–105
Options, 19–20
Oracle Corporation, 12, 31–32, 43, 50, 98, 145–146, 166–169, 170, 171, 172
Outcomes, confusing with inputs, 67–69
Overworked employees, 141–142
Ownership issues, 56

Packard, Dave, 43
Partnerships:
  with customers, 199–200
  of Diba, 175, 177–178, 179–180, 181, 184, 187
Performing phase, of project management, 108–110
Personality types, knowledge worker, 50–55
Pfeffer, Jeffrey, 21
Phillips, David, 48, 191

Plan/Do/Check/Act (PDCA) Productivity
Cycle, 102
Planning phase:
approval in, 108
budget for, 107
checklist for, 106
of project management, 105–108,
126–128
resources for, 107, 197
schedule for, 106–107
Portfolio management, 69, 70, 75–94
balancing the portfolio, 88–89, 94, 199
categorizing the work, 85–88, 94
collaboration and, 192, 196
defining the portfolio, 77–78, 94, 191–192
knowledge management and, 149
managing the portfolio, 89–90, 94
opportunity analysis in, 90–93, 102–105
payoff of, 93–94
prioritizing the portfolio, 79–84, 94
reviewing the portfolio, 78–79, 94, 192,
196
setting and communicating priorities,
76–77
transparency and, 191–192
(*See also* Priorities)
Press coverage, 181–182, 198
Price Waterhouse Coopers, 17
Priorities, 30–31, 33–34, 38, 75–94
business process, 117–120
identifying, 70, 72
working on the wrong projects as
problem of, 64, 69, 70
(*See also* Portfolio management)
Process group, 195–196
Process management, 34–35, 38, 70–71,
95–122, 196–199
best practices in, 70–71, 72, 116, 199
examples of, 95–98
nature of, 99–100
reinventing-the-wheel problem in,
65–66, 69, 70–71
types of processes, 100–101
(*See also* Business process; Project
management process)
Productivity:
Hawthorne effect and, 130–131, 134
of knowledge workers, 3–4, 10–11, 13, 15
of manual workers, 13
working smart and, 30, 36, 39
Program managers, 193–194, 195
Program office, 193–194
Progress tracking, 35, 39, 123–144
active management involvement in, 135,
144
baseline plan in, 126–128
closed-loop project control and, 109,
125–126, 138–139, 195, 196
cost of, 144

Progress tracking (*Cont.*):
dumptruck reports in, 66–67
flying-by-the-seat-of-your-pants project
control and, 125
going-through-the-motions scenario,
142–144
implementing, 71, 72–73
improvements to expect from, 131–132
knowledge management and, 161
management sensitivity to, 132–134
mechanics of, 137
pitfalls of, 128–131, 140–144
in portfolio management, 78–79, 80, 84
problems in, 66–67
program managers and, 193–194, 195
in project management, 108–110
real-world, 135–137
transparency and, 192–194
vague reports in, 66, 124–125
visibility and, 66–67, 69, 71, 131–132
Project Management Institute (PMI), 102,
195
Project management process, 22–23,
101–115
business process versus, 101
closing phase, 113–115, 197
correcting phase, 111–113
defined, 100
implementing, 120
initiation phase, 102–105, 126, 198–199
knowledge management and, 161
performing phase, 108–110
planning phase, 105–108, 126–128
simplicity in, 120–122
standardizing, 195–196
Public relations, 181–182, 198
Purpose of job, in Accountability Management System, 28–29, 38, 41–42, 45–47

Raspallo, David, 22, 95–97, 116
Read, Stuart, 171, 183, 184
Reinventing-the-wheel problem, 65–66,
69, 70–71
Rework rate, 132

Saba, Steve, 144
Schedule:
for planning phase, 106–107
updating, in progress tracking, 135, 136
Securities and Exchange Commission
(SEC), 34–35
Shared-services organization, 92
Simonson, Nancy, 142–144
Six Sigma Methodology, 114–115, 195
Skilling, Jeff, 1, 2
Soft benefits/savings, 82–83
Standardization, 195–196
Status reports, 78, 79, 108, 109, 120, 192
Stoutamore, Tim, 183

Strategy group, 198–199
Stroking, of knowledge workers, 23–24,
    44–45
Sun Microsystems, 165, 172, 188

T-Mobile, 66–67, 190
Tacit knowledge:
    nature of, 155–157
    sharing of, 157–158, 160–161, 199
Tandem Computer, 12, 168
Taxonomies, in knowledge management
    systems, 148, 153–154
Teamwork:
    importance of, 18
    knowledge management and, 149–150,
        156–159
    portfolio management and, 192
Technical knowledge, of knowledge workers,
    16–17
Textron Financial, 22, 95–97
Thompson, Peter, 90
Thomson, William (Lord Kelvin), 123
Time, accountability for, 19, 21–22,
    123–124, 132–134, 192–194 (See also
    Progress tracking)
Toxic knowledge workers, 21, 35, 63
Transparency, 189–200
    accountability management and, 5
    adult supervision and, 5, 63, 190–191
    big-picture approach to business,
        18–19
    corporate culture and, 190–191
    customer focus and, 199–200
    defined, 61
    emotional insight, 17
    as goal, 5
    lack of, 62
    portfolio management and,
        191–192
    process management and, 194–199
    progress tracking and, 192–194

Transparency (*Cont.*):
    testing the job market, 49, 54–55
    (*See also* Visibility)
Tribal knowledge, 96, 116
Truman, Harry, 41

Unilever, 190

Vague reports, 66, 124–125
Variance reports, 110, 111–113, 138–139,
    144
Venture capitalists, 17
Vieregge, Bernhard, 66–67
Visibility, 62–64
    confusing inputs and outcomes,
        67–69
    defined, 61
    nature of, 62–63
    progress tracking and, 66–67, 69, 71,
        131–132
    reinventing the wheel, 65–66, 69, 70–71
    warning signs concerning, 63–64
    working on the wrong projects, 64, 69,
        70

Wavetron Microsystems, 169
Webb, Maynard, 27, 28, 36–38, 199
WebEx, 150
Webvan, 2
Whelchel, Richard, 71–73, 113
Western Electric, 130–131
Wilkes, Jeremy, 17
Wolff, Greg, 173
Wong, Ted, 183
Work-life balance, 24–25, 58–60
Working smart, in Accountability
    Management System, 30, 36, 39

Yahoo, 2

Zenith, 175, 179, 181, 187

About the Authors

Farzad and Rhonda Dibachi are cofounders of Niku Corporation, an enterprise application software company.

Farzad has served as the chief executive officer and chairman of the board of directors of Niku since he cofounded the company in January 1998. Prior to Niku, Farzad was the cofounder, president, and CEO of Diba, an information appliance software startup company. He also worked at Oracle, Tandem, and GE. Farzad received a B.A. in Mechanical Engineering and Computer Science from San Jose State University and attended a graduate program at Santa Clara University.

Rhonda is the executive vice president of strategy and planning at Niku. Previously, she worked at Webvan, Oracle, Arthur Young (now Ernst & Young), and GE. Rhonda has a B.S.N.E. from Northwestern University and an M.B.A. from Santa Clara University.

Farzad and Rhonda have been married since 1989.